By the River

Essays from the Water's Edge

T0322545

By the River

Essays from the Water's Edge

DAUNT BOOKS

First published in the United Kingdom in 2024 by
Daunt Books
83 Marylebone High Street
London W1U 4QW

1

Typeset by Marsha Swan
Printed and bound by TJ Books Limited, Padstow, Cornwall
www.dauntbookspublishing.co.uk

Contents

Reading the River

Crossing the River

CONTENTS

Beyond the River

Reading the River

I Felt Sure She Had Gone Down to the River

JO HAMYA

Something compels me to work through her diaries in reverse chronological order. At my desk in the British Library, I flip a stack of five volumes over and read from the last page. What I do not want to say is there, relayed briefly as an editorial note by Anne Oliver Bell. 'The following morning Virginia drowned herself in the tidal river Ouse; Leonard found her stick on the bank near the swing bridge at Southease . . .'[1]

    I am aware of this already. It sits in my mind alongside the other mythos I began accumulating age thirteen, when I first saw her photo. A lot of it is composed of sad, beautiful women I know very little about. Nicole Kidman's prosthetic nose and brown housecoat sinking into the water. Florence Welch keening 'pockets full of stones' over harps and bass. Gillian Anderson's pellucid voice transmitted through speakers at the Royal Opera House reading, '*Dearest. . .*', while eighteen ballerinas lift their bodies in front of a twenty-one-minute-long video of black-and-white waves. These days, when I sit at my desk to write, there is a blue-and-grey postcard of George Charles Beresford's portrait of a twenty-year-old Woolf stuck onto the bookshelf beside me. It is the same image I first came upon of her. It is always there, in the corner of my eye. It is what hangs in everyone's eye: Virginia, young and beautiful and sombre, with her head tilted down. I have not spent as much time as I would like seeking to replace it with Vanessa Bell's painting of her sister, pink-lipped, knitting something red in a bright orange armchair.

Guilt dictates what I want to do with this essay – I want to imagine it as a river flowing backwards. How much have I allowed myself to know about her? Suppose she'd never walked into the water. What would I have to write about then?

On Tuesday 5 November 1940, Woolf was fifty-eight, and settled in Rodmell, East Sussex. She had grown used to German planes flying overhead, as had Leonard. Later in life, he recalls for his autobiography, 'the swishing of bombs overhead and ... the dull explosions towards the River Ouse'.[2]

That previous Saturday, one of those bombs breached the river's banks, with subsequent rain and high tide allowing the water to rise to the bottom of the Woolfs' garden. This, Virginia recorded in her diary. *The haystack in the floods is of such incredible beauty ... When I look up I see all the marsh water. In the sun deep blue, gulls caraway seeds: snowberries[?]: Atlantic flier: yellow islands: leafless trees: red cottage roofs. Oh may the flood last forever ...* She does not seem to mind that it has robbed her, temporarily, of her walks by the marsh and the banks, where craters of unexploded bombs lay marked with white wooden crosses. She is alive to colour and detail wherever it can be found. *I have never been so fertile*, reads one passage.[3] And a month previously, on examining those white crosses, *I don't want to die yet.*[4]

'I don't want to die yet' – but in that same entry, she can picture it perfectly. *I've got it fairly vivid – the sensation: but cant see anything but suffocating nonentity following after. I shall think – oh I wanted another 10 years – not this – & shant for once, be able to describe it. It – I mean death; no, the scrunching & scrambling, the crushing of my bone shade in on my very active eye & brain: the process of putting out the light, – painful? Yes. Terrifying. I suppose so – Then a swoon; a drum; two or three gulps attempting consciousness – & then, dot dot dot.*[5]

Should too much of our cultural imagination be preoccupied with beautified fashionings of Woolf's death, it may well be because, whether through illness, or two world wars, Woolf herself was not immune to the same impulse. Still, not long after finishing my research I come across an article from the *Guardian*, titled, 'River Ouse may become first in England to gain legal rights'. Such rights, it explains, are likely to be based on the Universal Declaration of River Rights, 'which says rivers should have the right to flow, perform essential functions within the river's ecosystem, be free from pollution ... have native biodiversity, as well as the right to regeneration and restoration'.[6] I think carefully over what I have read, and find I have not been attentive enough. *It – I mean death; no –* 'no'. When Virginia thinks about death, more often than not, she is disgruntled at the thought of not being able to live, and more importantly, describe living – *the scrunching and scrambling.* In her final note to Leonard, death is justified through the loss of some of the greatest pleasures she took in life: *I can't concentrate ... I can't even write this properly. I can't read.*

Monk's House at Rodmell still looks out at Mount Caburn. It is separated from the South Downs by the Ouse, and visible from the windows of the Woolfs' cottage. From 1919 to 1939, the area served as a holiday retreat for the couple. Mentions of the river occur frequently in Virginia's diaries. Over the years, she records its colour faithfully, by turns sky blue, or lead, or silver. She notes kingfishers with bright orange or chocolate undersides, stoats with white-tipped tails.[7] She worries over local building developments, which she fears will impair the environment and surrounding streams of water, grousing, for all her metropolitan affect, at the thought of *that hideous new house on top of my down; the rampart so often looked at on my evening walk. They are building a garage now . . .*[8]

I try very hard to picture all of this.

Virginia, the nosy neighbour.

Virginia, distempered and spying on others – like any other woman in a small town, like people I have known and spoken with at various points in my life. With her walking stick and her hat, meditating in the morning, meditating in the afternoon, while taking her daily stroll. Once she has moved to Monk's House for good, she expresses a desire for her diary to *conglobulate reflections like Gide.* The trouble is there's never a pen at hand when her mind springs to work pleasurably, and unbidden; whatever she might write *occur*[s] . . . *when I'm up to my knees in mud. The lost thoughts – a fine covey they'd make if ever hived – the thoughts I've lost on Asheham down, & walking the river bank.* In a way, this is not surprising. More than anything, her proximity to rivers seems to signal a time in which she can relinquish stress, or insecurity; become someone ordinary and unburdened – think, freely. On Monday 12 November 1934, she is procrastinating rewriting *The Years*, she is being persuaded to write *The Life of Roger Fry*. She wonders *What . . . I feel about it – If I could be free, then there's the chance* – so walks *to Piddinghoe, & back by the river. And my brain rose out of the mist . . . I felt young & vigorous.*

In motion is my favourite state to find Woolf during the course of her diaries. She is, unreservedly, a social creature, even when she tries to be morbid. *I meant to write about death, only life came breaking in as usual . . . I have taken it into my head that I shan't live till 70. Suppose, I said to myself the other day this pain over my heart suddenly wrung me out like a dish cloth & left me dead? – I was feeling sleepy, indifferent, & calm; & so thought it didn't much matter, except for L. Then, some bird or light I daresay, or waking wider, set me off wishing . . . chiefly to walk along the river & look at things.*[9]

By June of 1919, the Woolfs had acquired the Round House in East Sussex. It had been bought in a burst of false optimism. It *no longer seemed so radiant & unattainable when examined* by the pair as owners, rather than prospective buyers; Woolf thought her husband *a little disappointed, though just & polite even to its merits.* She herself criticised the bedrooms, which were very small, *the garden — not a country garden.* But that previous Thursday, on a walk from the station to inspect their new lodgings, the couple *read out a placard stuck on the auctioneers wall. Lot 1. Monks House, Rodmell. An old fashioned house standing in three quarters of an acre of land to be sold with possession.* 'That would have suited us exactly' L. said.

On paper, Woolf flatters herself a born–again realist after the disappointment of their recent purchase. In early July, she cycles against strong wind to gather details regarding the other house. *Monks are nothing out of the way,* she quips, and lists its many flaws. The kitchen is *distinctly bad.* Although there is an oil stove, it has no grate. The rooms are small; there is no hot water; no baths. But there is purple samphire on the lawn, a sense of shelter in the long, low form of the house. It is not a place of ceremony or precision. It shelters. It comforts. Woolf delights with profound pleasure at *the size & shape & fertility & wildness of the garden.* She sees quickly how easily Leonard would take to caring for the *infinity of fruitbearing trees; the plums crow[d]ed so as to weigh the tip of the branch down.* There are cabbages and *well kept rows of peas, artichokes, potatoes; raspberry bushes [with] pale little pyramids of fruit* to nourish the couple. Despite only just having bought a house nearby, the Woolfs resolve to go to auction.

I don't suppose many spaces of five minutes in the course of my life have been so close packed with sensation, Virginia recalls. The auction took place at the White Heart. The room was crowded. £800 is as high as they can go, the couple decides, and that being established, Virginia organises her husband into line. *Does he look as if he had £800 in his pocket?* she wonders, and frets at what the other farmers in the room might offer as a result. But the first call comes in: £300. *Not an offer,* the auctioneer says firmly, and begins the bid afresh. This time £400, and the sum rises too quickly for Woolf's taste in aggregates of fifty to £600 before the room lulls. Four buyers drop out. With six left, the bids slow to amounts of *twenties; then tens; then fives,* until just short of £700, the auctioneer raises his hammer one last time. Virginia is purple in the cheeks and Leonard trembles like a reed. *The solid fact,* she rejoices, *is that we own, besides the Round House, Monks House at Rodmell, with three quarters of an acre of land. We own Monks House (this is almost the first time I've written a name which I hope to write many thousands of times before I've done with it) for ever.*[10]

Here, then, is one way to look at Woolf's life, so much of it spent profitably in her country home. Fifty-five, and refreshed by *a hot sulphurous week end* in Rodmell, where red grass reached up her knees and covered her as she lay by the riverbank with Leonard.[11] Fifty-two, and justifying the expense of hiring a small boat for herself and her nephew visiting from Charleston: the pleasure at *wallop[ing] about on the river*.[12] Summer in Sussex at forty-seven, in thick shoes on her daily walk by the water after a lunch of rissoles and chocolate custard.[13] Forty-six, and jostling guests out of her cottage to the marsh – she comes across charmingly despondent after: *sorry the river was low, or they might have praised it*.[14] A year earlier, spread out in the freshly done garden at Monk's House, watching the new terrace be built, and reflecting on a walk by the water with Vita while *The Waves* – then titled *The Moths* – began to take shape in her mind: *I think I will write quickly; It is to be a love story: she is finally to let the last great moth in. The contrasts might be something of this sort: she might talk, or think, about the age of the earth: the death of humanity: then moths keep on coming*.[15] Virginia, consoling herself over the slow progress of *To the Lighthouse* with *washing in boundless warm fresh air* over the downs.[16] In her diaries, an endless supply of material in which she reads Byron, and Marryat, grouses over unwanted, or unexpected visitors interrupting her workflow. She puzzles out *Mrs Dalloway*, walks friends' dogs, delights in ordering silk dresses – all at Rodmell, all by the Ouse.

In the fifth volume of his autobiography, Leonard Woolf comes, finally, to his wife's death. Despite the urging of friends, he has not left Monk's House and the memories it holds. He does not dwell on what happened for very long. She had gone missing. Little time had elapsed since he had read a draft of *Between the Acts*, and 'even four days before her suicide [Virginia] could be thinking of writing another book.' 'I felt sure,' he concludes, 'that she had gone down to the river.'[17]

The Harbour

AMY KEY

Whenever I see the sea barge into the river, I find it disturbing. *You're going the wrong way!* I want to shout. The surface of the water rugged and rapid, like an endless crumpled, pulled-back sheet. It wears its resistance. My mum and I sit and watch as if we're at the cinema. The river rises and fills the enormous screen of the living-room window.

The water calms. Every now and then I say *oh, I think there's a seal*, believing I can see a head bob up above the water. Mum gets her binoculars. *I'm sorry, love, that's just a piece of wood, I think.* Or just as easily an empty plastic container. It does happen, though. Seals, dolphins too, sometimes. I have a little video Mum sent us all, the lovely curving leap, a slinky on the water.

Mum's flat is situated on the south of the Tyne, looking across the river to the Fish Quay in North Shields. Twice a day you can watch an enormous cruise liner enter and exit. Slip out from the confines of river into the lawless North Sea. Or the opposite. It goes from North Shields to Amsterdam and back again, 275 miles – so tantalisingly close! People wave from the deck. I always wave back. The ship is mammoth. It seems preposterous something so huge could be buoyant. *What can I learn from the ship*, I wonder. Maybe it is a kind of faith? The water and ship will perform their collaborative magic of flotation. Laws of physics, engineering, centuries of experimentation, innovation and intuition make it possible to travel on the water. I don't need to know the science to enjoy its effects, either as passenger or spectator. The ship floats as my body floats.

Tynemouth Pier on the north bank faces South Shields pier, like trees growing towards each other from opposite sides of the road, not yet touching. Tynemouth is posher than South Shields. We have a 2000-year-old Roman fort, Arbeia, but it's not visible from the harbour. In 1988 a Saturday morning TV show filmed there and the boyband Bros played, the producers invited local schoolkids to attend and I – already a devoted Bros fan – was among them. Tynemouth has the ruins of a medieval priory and castle, which you can see from my mum's flat; it also has big houses I was told were 'very expensive', and, in a renovated church, a grand shopping arcade with antiques shops, boutiques and a café. But I always enjoy that from South Shields we get that lovely dramatic view of the north, as well as our own beautiful beaches that become wilder and then more formal again as the coast creeps towards Sunderland. In addition to our own pier, which is almost a mile long – so impressive for such a small town – we have the stubby Groyne pier with its bright red lighthouse. You can see it from my mum's patio, a hot throb at the edge of your vision.

Sometimes the weather is so bad, the water so rough, you can see huge waves crash over Tynemouth Pier, magnificent white waves smashing up and over the brickwork, like a waterfall in reverse. I love watching the water, but the river has always felt like something to be admired from a respectful distance. I recently found out, while researching my family tree, that my great-great-uncle John Urwin Key died in the river, in 1928, the year that construction was completed on the Tyne Bridge. He worked in a timber yard at Tyne Dock, South Shields's port. Travelling either to or from work, a tugboat had got too close to the 'sculler' boat he was on and caused water to flood its deck. He was washed overboard. He was twenty years old. Of the three children the Key family had, two – John and

Robert – died in water. John in the river, and Robert in the sea before him, at war. The third, a girl called Mabel, was left to mourn. I know this because I have Mabel's diary, which records her survivor's guilt, her wretched thought that she 'should have been drowned like other May kittens'. She felt her life was worth less than those of her brothers, and she should be gone in their place. A girl's life was less valuable, especially a working-class girl's life, and she knew it.

There's a story behind the one the river offers me in a purely sensory way – where its power is revealed through observation, exposure to its elements, keen listening. It's a story the river created, a turbulent, multi-generational historical epic; the economic legend of the place that was once home. Lately I've been watching videos of people who used to work on the Tyne, or whose parents did. They remember the enthusiastic industry of the river, a river that kept families fed and men in work. In one, a man called Duncan Stephenson spoke on film about how when he was fifteen he was approached to work on the Tyne; 'can you scull?', he was asked by a tugboat man ('scull' meaning 'row'), who recruited him as a 'tugboat lad'. He remembered there were forty tugs working night and day, and now there were only three working tugs on the Tyne. 'Breaks my heart to see it'; Stephenson says, in the video. 'The ship-ping industry fled, they're building houses now where they used to build ships.' But I know this isn't my story to tell – I reach back to the past because I want to claim it, but I can't. Outside my mum's flat there are the remains of wooden staithes in the water, where boats were moored, or loaded, unloaded.

My family moved from Deal in Kent to South Shields in 1987, when I was nine. We left the place where Mum grew up and went to the place where my dad grew up, swapped one east coast for another further up the country. It's a long time since I've lived there – twenty-six years – but it's hard not to call *home* the place where a parent lives, even when the family home is long gone, its members scattered.

When I was at school in South Shields, while I believed in my own brand of cool (I liked indie music, I read books, had older pen pals who lived in big cities, had been to see Huggy Bear and Bikini Kill play at a nightclub!), within the hierarchy of school clans I was in The Swots. During lunchbreak, while my classmates would be outside, playing games or at the nearby shops, I would spend time in the school's music room, eating lunch with my friends. This was my music teacher's classroom where he and the drama teacher set out an elaborate picnic for themselves each day, with 'French stick', Boursin and a box of red wine. The wine gave the room an intoxicating air of mild rebellion. We were proximate to getting drunk. My friends and I would decant our packed lunches and try to secure ourselves a piano (there was a grand and an electric) so we could practise whatever song we were writing or learning at that time. We might have been insufferable but at least, in this room, we were safe to be so.

A song we were taught in choir, and which we would rehearse in the music room, was 'Waters of Tyne', an old Northumbrian folk song. It was arranged by my music teacher in three-part harmony. When I think of it, I hear his low groaning tenor 'ahhh' from the introduction, a base note from which our young female voices sprung upwards. The song as I was taught it is sung from the perspective of a young woman pining for her sweetheart who lives over the water. With tears in her eyes, she sings for a boatman to 'scull' her love over the 'rough river'. It had the ardent romantic drama that teenage me lived for. I had to sing the alto part, enjoying how my voice moved between the high and low vibrations; I was able to exist in a safe channel, boundaried by voices on trickier paths. A tugboat guiding a ship into the river. I had an idealised, nostalgic image of the Tyne, as a rough river that kept lovers apart, a broad, mercurial medium for longing. Different viewpoints exist about the setting for the 'Waters of Tyne' but the lyrical reference to a river being rough made me believe it can only take place close to the harbour, precisely where my mum lives now.

Lots of north-eastern musicians have recorded a version of 'Waters of Tyne' but I've never found a version I like more than the way we sang it at school, unaccompanied. Now, when I listen to it in my head, knowing how John died in the Tyne, I wish I knew how Mabel felt about the river, wish she'd written about it. I want to know if she knew the song, and if she did, was she ever able to sing it again, to the rough waters of Tyne that kept her from her beloved brother?

To get to South Shields from London by train you first must cross the Tyne, then cross back again. From the train, after you curve out from an enclosure – maybe a tunnel – the Tyne Bridge appears on the right, obscured by the other bridges: the swing bridge, high level, the bright blue metro bridge. A beloved face seen through a crowd. My head always turns sharply towards the bridges, intent on the symbols of homecoming, the Tyne Bridge being the ultimate one. In a car, driving back over the river towards South Shields, the Tyne is a thread to my left, even when I cannot see it. It is a thread in my mind, even when I am not home, a kind of anchor – a gathering point for family.

Mum lives off a road called River Drive. In our family group chat, she shares photos of the grey days, the peach melba sunsets, the surprise of snow that has settled, updates on her hanging baskets and roses, the animal life of the harbour. Whenever any of us visit we drift out of conversation, attention pulled into the river. Our photo rolls fill up with images of the same view, same mood as all the times before. Fishermen are sometimes right outside Mum's door. They set up camp on the bricked walkway; fold-out chairs, a small pop-up tent. Once there was a whole family who brought a stereo and had a party. I thought Mum would lose it, but they packed up and left when it started to get dark. She doesn't see the fishers having much success – some dinks here and there.

When I'm there I like to step outside to the riverside when it's dark. It's a cleansing kind of air, a cold silk to it. I like to see what the moon is up to, to see how it has altered the river. I sit at my mum's little café table, on a cool metal chair, and watch the river at the point it meets the sea.

I like knowing that whatever the river is doing when I go to sleep, by the time I wake all will be different. It's a sluice for the brain. I don't need it to be placid and blue, or raucous and grey. Sometimes you can't even see the river, the fog obscures everything. The river is a ghost – pure vapour – you have to take for granted is there. I feel similarly about my ancestry, about what ties us together. There's that saying about rivers – you can never step into the same one twice.

It's never the same river and you're never the same person stepping into it. I like that idea, but a river is more than the water passing through it. And I can't help but think of how me, my family, my north-eastern ancestors, all know, knew, the Tyne. Me, Mum, Dad, in the end both sets of grandparents, Mabel, John, my siblings, nieces and nephews, every little branch on the northern tree. It's something we've shared, a prevailing connective tissue. I take for granted something connects us beyond DNA. Another anchor. The tide will go out and the tide will come back in. The river will be there even if you cannot see it. But I find it strange to think about how of all those family members, it's my mum who is left in South Shields. My mum, who came from the south, is the last one standing. She's the one who has made the Tyne her own. She both lives in the harbour and is the harbour.

When we moved to the north as a family, we lived behind the Town Hall, which has a staggering grandeur for a place that is now so economically challenged. My hours were kept by the Town Hall clock, which may as well have been Big Ben as far I was concerned. I didn't go down to the river much, but we would walk ten minutes down the road to the sea where the arcades were, where boys on skateboards would be. The river was something to be crossed rather than looked at. But many years after my parents divorced, and long after

I'd left for London, my mum fell in love with a man who lived with a view of the harbour.

She moved from our family home to live with him and together they conspired to buy the flat next door to his so that my elderly grandparents could move from Deal to South Shields, and my mum would be able to look after them. She and her partner Malcolm and my grandparents lived side by side. In their respective homes, they would sit in their pairs at the window and look out onto the river. When I visited, I loved sliding the back door open from Mum's and popping into my grandparents', calling out a cheery 'hello!' I think of my grandma saying of the river, 'it's better than the TV!' I can hear her when I look. We're connected by our fascination with the river. Or more accurately, the river as it meets the sea, where the voyage out and the homecoming collide.

My grandparents are now dead; last year Malcolm died too. My mum lives in the flat my grandparents lived in, next door to the place she and Malcolm lived. When I visit, I get to feel reminded of them, but I worry for my mum that perhaps the harbour accommodates other feelings, of painful loss, of abandonment. I wonder what the river means for her, this sense of love coming and going, of her being the only constant.

I've never followed the river further than Newcastle; I've never encountered the point where its two main tributaries – the North and South Tyne rivers – meet in a tranquil spot with its bright, pebbled shore thirty miles inland. The river's end, its thrusting out into the sea, is all that matters to me. I sit on Mum's patio, whatever the weather. I try to commit the view to memory each time because I want to place my mum there, to borrow her eyes and see what she sees. Every day, I know she looks out to the River Tyne and then to the sea. I know she'll be considering whether the sunset will be good tonight, whether the wind has dropped enough for her to have her tea outside, whether it's a good time to tend to her hanging baskets and riverside roses. I like thinking of her there, knowing the quality of light, the engrossing drama of it. I retreat into the safe harbour of her perspective. I think of the river, and my mum is held there.

Memory River

MARCHELLE FARRELL

A stream runs through our garden. It is no river, but one of the many small points that form the tributaries of a larger body. Water wells from underground. It runs constantly down the steep slopes of the garden; has never dried up in our years of being here. It is clean and clear, full of tiny freshwater shrimp and larvae, and babbles cheerfully. At one point in its course, a succession of small waterfalls and pools were created by a previous inhabitant, a feature that lives on as a permanent reminder of lives past. The water cascades down them, a replica in miniature of the tropical waterfalls of my childhood home that I would visit on hikes, jump over on exhilarating rope swings, and into whose green-gold spangled pools I would dive. The tiny falls in my garden are a playground for robins, the fairies of my daughter's imagination and a solitary, reticent goldfish that we were surprised to discover in one of the pools a couple of months after moving in.

Sometimes I look at the cool water emerging from a bank under the roots of an ash tree and it strikes me as magical. I understand why so many have worshipped springs and rivers over time, why a dip in the never-ending eddy rising from some unseen source might be seen as healing or offering renewal. The fresh flow of water brings life, our planet a blue-green oasis in a desert galaxy. My mind was parched and barren when we found this place, and it was the vibrant song of the stream and the spring from which it arose that called me to settle here. Something in the flow of water has freed the tide of memory and unleashed a deluge of forgotten stories. The verdant garden that I grow along the water's course, and the stories that it evokes in me, have recalled me to myself; the act of rooting my existence at this river's origin has re-infused me with creative life.

I grew up in the foothills of the Northern Range in Trinidad, the birthplace of the St Ann's River. A river which had been bled dry, diverted by a colonial governor long-dead so that the streets of Port of Spain could be built upon its flood-plain banks. The not-so-new waterway created in its place has a name that is telling: East Dry River. The wide concrete banks created to contain a torrent, so that a city might rise out of a marsh, nowadays tend to hold a mere trickle. The way the streets still overflow in heavy rains shows how the water wants to remember its own place.

A paved drain that marks the old watercourse winds from lower Port of Spain up towards the valley that holds the neighbourhood of my childhood. In heavy rains some water would sit in the ditch, which is all that remains of a once sweet river. Come dry season on the hottest days, the stagnant puddles would stink. I wondered if the undisturbed St Ann's River of centuries past reeked in the lush paintings of Michel-Jean Cazabon, bamboo gracefully arching over the water's natural curves. Smell is a direct portal to memory but there is none in old photos or paintings. No scratch-'n'-sniff visceral pull to an embodied past. Instead, there are only the stories we wish to keep telling ourselves, misremembered untruths in their edited cleanliness.

The St Ann's River had not been diverted up on the slopes of my childhood, but largely unregulated development had changed the water's flow anyway. The mostly empty riverbed divided two suburbs in the foothills to the north of Port of Spain. Cascade, the home of the middle class; St Ann's, the home of what was colloquially known as the madhouse, whose inhabitants could be seen walking down the streets towards town from time to time. The psychiatric hospital was in the style of an old-fashioned asylum. Tall gates, beautiful grounds, institutionalised patients. The river that curved past the old wrought-iron gates and my home may have run dry, but something had been carved through the everyday flow of those moments, into the bedrock of my consciousness. It washed me downstream to the sea, carried me on currents across the Atlantic and through medical school, and eventually deposited me on the shores of a psychiatric career.

We tend to think of the way the mind works as linear. In our everyday constraints of screens and concrete, we apply the theories that we think we know to try to understand the machine of the mind. We reduce ourselves to the equivalent of the inanimate objects that we produce. But in my hours of sitting in quiet, intimate rooms attempting to shine a light of understanding into the disturbed murk that can emerge to obscure the psyche of others, it became clear that, of course, our minds are akin to – kin with – the living world we inhabit. I have come to see the inner world as a landscape.

This internal domain takes shape as we do, through relationship with the living terrain that holds and moulds, and nurtures and harms, and makes us. We wander through it over a lifetime: sometimes getting stuck in chasms from which it seems there could be no escape, sometimes spending years seeming to circle the same ground. An arid inner landscape is a desolate scene, on which little growth flourishes.

Memory flows like a river, and it is through its constant flow that we come into being. We live in the moment: the ever-changing, ever-forward-rushing current of now. The flow of experience, once retained, constantly reshapes the land of self through which it courses, forming bedrock, and depositing the mud of new, fertile ground. A featureless plain becomes a richly textured topography of ridges and valleys, cliffs and plateaus, clothed in earth in which all manner of relationships can take root.

Without memory, we have no self. We see this clearly once it is lost, such as when the person leaves the living body behind in advanced dementia. Emotional disturbance goes hand in hand with disruptions in memory: the entire field of psychoanalysis was founded on a recognition of the things too painful to consciously remember that our unconscious cannot forget. Our DNA carries the molecular memory of what has gone before, downstream, through generations. We are built from living memory.

It is the foundation of our humanity; the erosion of the ability to remember themselves, through being stripped of language, culture, relationship and expression of spirituality, all the forms of storytelling that weave the tapestry of life, was a crucial way in which my enslaved ancestors came to be subjugated and controlled. It was how we came to almost lose consciousness of who we really are.

My children are English, but I am Trinidadian. To teach them something of who I am, I took them home for carnival. Every year people pour from the surrounding hills and valleys and onto the streets of Port of Spain and follow the music, to form rivers of drinking, dancing merrymakers participating in the ritual of the mas. Carnival: now taking the form of weeks of celebration culminating in a two-day street party, with its origins in the wellsprings of resistance and rebellion when enslaved people mocked their captors' Lenten festivities, or covered themselves in black molasses and carried torches to celebrate the constant uprisings and burning of the cane fields that were the site of so much suffering. Carnival: born as an act of memory, a way to remember dignity and humanity, to transcend suffering and rediscover joy. It lives on as a bodily reminiscence: every year's bacchanal flooding the streets of Port of Spain, a mass renewal.

My parents had moved away from St Ann's to a neighbourhood with no rivers, but in order to be close to the festivities we all stayed at a hotel in the hills I recollected so well. We walked down the pavement that followed the dried-up St Ann's River into town, and once there, in the centre of it all, I watched as my children immersed themselves in the flow of carnival. I saw them shift and change, so malleable still, as the soil of their selves was shaped by the buffeting currents of revelry around them. At first, they watched wide-eyed, then they began to dance and sing to the rhythms that their cells must remember, their limbs joyfully picked up and washed along by the tides of old stories recalled anew in their young bodies.

One afternoon during a quiet pause I found myself showing the children photos and videos of their past selves, which they love to see. A past that still feels quite close to me: the folds of soft thighs, gummy grins and fists tightly clasped around my fingers. But worlds long distant to them; they edged each other out of the way to put their heads in front of my hand, a constant motion of gangly limbs lightly shoving, interrupted by gap-toothed cackles at the antics of a baby onscreen.

Watching their delight as we scrolled through captured moments on my phone, my father remarked that he wished he had taken more photos of me in my childhood. We had been reminiscing about school holiday trips to the village of Blanchisseuse on the north coast of Trinidad, where one of my favourite things to do was to swim from the suspension bridge over the Marianne River to meet the sea. Usually, I would be alone. Waved off by one parent, met by the other on the beach. Sometimes I would be poled downstream by village boys who had made rafts from lengths of bamboo lashed together with rope. Massive groves dotted the river's edge, arching over the water's mirror-like surface, trying to reach the palm and sea almond trees on the opposite bank. It was a cathedral nave more glorious than any that human hands had tried to render in marble and stone.

Often, memories of floating on my back along a hidden current feel like a dream. Precious only daughter of otherwise cautious parents, did I really dive off the bridge into Mama D'Leau's waters, rumoured to be rich in caiman, unaccompanied? Mama D'Leau was the mother goddess of the rivers, healer and protector of the creatures of her watery realm; my childhood innocence made me one of them. My father also holds these dream-like memories, regrets that he did not capture these fragments of time onto fragile celluloid. Part of me wishes he had, witnessing my children's glee in this remarkable thing of being able to see into the past. But I am also glad that they only live in the vivid technicolour of our shared recollection, in the stories of my adventures that we weave, and in the many rich layers of memory and relationship that form our selves. I wonder who I would be if I did not remember those days. A woman more afraid of taking a plunge of faith into the unknown.

The Marianne River of my childhood memory is wide and deep, a still surface hiding the strong current that steadily flowed from the Northern Range to the sea. I take my children to swim in it, and in that river's cousin, the Grand Riviere, another waterway that flows from the hills of the Northern Range to the remote northern coast of Trinidad. We start at the mouth of the river, and I watch as they swim upstream, until their heads are tiny dots bobbing on a mirror of deep green. I take photos of them immersed in the river of water, as I took photos of them absorbed in the flow of carnival, for us to remember these moments, when we return to our garden, perhaps looking at them on a hot summer's day while dipping our toes in the stream.

Back at home in England, our little rivulet makes its way from our garden into the local brook, which eventually joins the river Avon, to finally meet the sea at the Severn Estuary. The port city of Bristol was built up around the mouth of the estuary, partly because of its important role in the transatlantic slave trade. My husband was born in Bristol: the city is part of my children's heritage, its history passed down on both sides. It is thought that the city's traders brought over half a million Africans into slavery in the Caribbean, perhaps including some of my ancestors. I do not know for certain. We have no record of them. In the loss of their living memory, they have been annihilated, rendered worse than dead.

I speak these tales into memory for my children, in the hope that healing stories will recall us to the full possibility of our vibrant selves. They do not understand yet, but I see how the flow of my words begins to shape the terrain of their minds. I hope they will remember them, as they will recall the times when we went swimming in the wide, deep rivers of the northern coast of Trinidad. I keep records of these events. But for now, I put down my phone, and submerge myself in the river with the children, as we laughingly allow the lively current to carry us to meet the blood-warm amniotic sea.

An Orange Vision

REBECCA MAY JOHNSON

For Susie, Forever

Half awake, I have a vision. Every few steps on a walk through the woods are interrupted by a flash of colour. Then the colour freezes, melts, and runs down in drips until it covers the landscape and river running through it. The view ahead is flooded by orange.

A few days later at the MoMA in New York I see an image that unexpectedly and intensely returns me to that orange vision, in an exhibition of sketches and watercolours by Georgia O'Keeffe. It is one in a series of drawings that at first glance look like the trees, with wider sections resembling a trunk with smaller narrow branches. Faint biro sketches on pieces of hotel note-paper develop into larger, darker drawings that are carefully shaded with a pencil or charcoal. Then, becoming radiant, the trunk and branches are rendered in colour, backlit first by an orange-yellow colour (*It Was Yellow and Pink II*), and then red (*It Was Yellow and Pink III*). When I move closer and read the information cards, I see that the pictures are O'Keeffe's depictions of rivers as seen from a plane: *Untitled (Abstraction/River)*, 1959. Rivers become trees become rivers.

The crooked lines of O'Keeffe's tributaries remind me of the wiggly branches of stunted oaks growing along the shores of the River O, where I spend every summer of my childhood. When I walk under their canopy the pungent salinity of seaweed and rotting crabs and washed-up jellyfish and the muddy riverbed at low tide and pig shit on the breeze and the sweet earth among the ferns is punctuated by intense flashes of orange. Then orange becomes the whole horizon – the object towards which most of my thoughts are directed when I am a child. As I walk along the river, I am thinking of an orange Calippo ice-lolly. The walk along the river to buy the ice-cream can feel interminably long as a child, but now I see it is very beautiful, snaking through woodland, emerging onto sunny sandy planes, crossing over small bridges, through leafy tunnels of green and views across the water and flat eastern landscape opening up intermittently.

In the summers by the river my brothers, our friends and I spend our days meditating on how we can get ice-cream and which of the adults we can convince to give us money to buy ice-cream from the various shops that sell it. There are two places with a freezer cabinet: one is a shop selling parts for boats near the caravan site where we stay and the other is a small gift shop downriver in a village where a famous author used to live and whose pub and resident barges appear in the paintings of many painters of rural scenes. We assess the best times to ask adults for ice-cream money, their various approaches to treats, and when they think treats should be eaten. We manage to get an ice-cream at least once on most days.

Eating a Calippo is frustrating but exciting and involves different methods as time goes on. Initially, when it's at its most frozen I chew tentatively on the icy top using my back teeth (my front teeth are too sensitive for this). As the temperature rises and it becomes softer, I become bolder and suck on the ice to extract the most flavouring I can. The lower section in its cardboard tube melts as I gnaw on the icy top and my reward is to drink the melted cold sweet nectar in the bottom. Sometimes I sort of mash up the thinner, lower half of the lolly in its tube with my hands so that I can enjoy the second half of the Calippo as a kind of slushy. The taste that I am so obsessed with is just sharp enough to prevent it becoming sickly sweet, and tastes vividly of orange.

Images of time spent alongside the river return to me often but I have trouble articulating their importance. Recently, the beloved mother of the siblings with whom I spent all my youth by the river died and remembering feels urgent. An unexpected encounter with a sketch of waves by O'Keeffe helps me to find a way. The reason I went to the MoMA and saw her orange river in the first place is that I came across pencil drawings of waves by O'Keeffe at another gallery: while walking through town my friend remembers that she likes The Drawing Center. They have a show about mythic worlds that includes a pencil drawing of waves by O'Keeffe. No contextualising scenery or colour confirms *Untitled (Abstraction)* as water, but the lines race upwards on the page like a river when it swells in high wind against tide. I feel the flutter of recognition, of being by the river when the wind is rising. I become caught up in O'Keeffe as if I have fallen into a river, carried by its flow. The waves are so alive that I keep re-seeing them after we leave the gallery, and they press me to see more of O'Keeffe's images.

By luck (or fate? – it feels like fate) the exhibition 'To See Takes Time' opens the day before I leave New York so I go and see it in the hour I have before catching the train. Early on I am struck by a pencil drawing of a tent door. The line is rough, as if O'Keeffe is looking at her object as she draws and following the rumpled fabric. Some lines are attempted twice, none is rubbed away. There is a faint hint of a tent pole bisecting the door but the dominant shape, marked in heavier lines, is the suggestive triangular opening. The tent door is explored via repetition and O'Keeffe introduces colour. She sees it again and again in blue that is bright and pale, then darkening to near black, and shades of deep red appear and brighten. The tent series wavers between representation and abstraction, it is memory where linear narrative is interrupted by vivid but opaque feeling. There is so much in the colour. Blue is a sky, is idealism, is clarity, is sinister, is clinical, is the unconscious. The reddened triangle is blood, a pink cunt, is passion, is a red sun shining through canvas at sunset, is the red mist of anger. O'Keeffe shows colour as mysterious language and asks what it is to really see something, to see it again and again. In *The Artist's Voice* she says 'there's nothing abstract about those pictures; they are what I saw – and very realistic to me'.

Her repetitions show me how to dwell with images that return. The tent series brings back a night in a tent during a lightning storm over the River O in early adolescence. I am in the tent with two sisters that I have known all my life. The tent is pitched in the woodland at the top of an earth cliff next to the river and is surrounded by the caravans in which our families sleep. We look out of the tent door to see branches of white light appear and disappear in the sky, a cinema of light and thunder rolls. We discuss being struck by lightning: there is evidence of it having happened locally. I have recently been told that the actual house where the famous author used to live was struck by lightning *only one mile* downriver. Walking the mile from where we are to the house seems far, but lightning can cover such distances like it's nothing. Apparently it burned a hole through the roof. I have not seen a picture but I imagine a blackened hole in the red roof tiles and a few burnt timbers showing through, maybe the sight of some furniture inside. What would it be like to be in a house when it's struck by lightning? A scenario I often consider as a child is what I would do if I were on the toilet when a disaster strikes. Would I pull up my trousers and run? I imagine the scale of emergency it would take to overcome my need for privacy in that situation. It feels necessary to work out my plan of action before the critical moment arrives.

In the thin-walled intimacy of the tent the older sister tells us about giving a blowjob to her boyfriend. The word 'blowjob' turns out to be appropriately vulgar in sound but not entirely accurate in meaning in terms of what she goes on to describe. I add it to the list of acts I would not want to be performing when lightning strikes. The boyfriend in question, who had recently visited us down by the river, is short in height and the most muscular person I have seen in real life. He is very clean and fastidiously groomed and he has a spotless, souped-up car with an exhaust that is amplified. He drives the younger sister and me up and down the road that runs down to the river to amuse us. He doesn't talk much, he is sweet. He is different to most of the men we know. The tent sits on the hard summer earth among the insects and the weather and is expressive of our semi-feral riverside existence. In sleeping bags we are close enough to hear each other breathe, our hair is stiff with saltwater from the river, and we scratch mosquito bites, which feels nice then painful as they begin to bleed. We discuss our imminent annihilation by lightning bolt against the distant sound of metal shrouds clanging on the masts of boats as the wind picks up. The tent is green, the tent is red, the tent is black like night, the tent is lit up by blinding white. We fall asleep.

In the morning we are listening to the birds in the trees above when the smell of garlic drifts in from the caravan in which the sisters' family are staying. We slide grubby feet into sandals and walk over to where the smell is coming from, a few metres away. Their mum is cooking mushrooms she has picked for breakfast. She is deeply knowledgeable about what is edible in hedges, fields and woods, and produces magnificent spreads with ingredients that she has foraged or grown. If her cupboard is bare: no it's not. My friend tells me that when they are in the car her mum pulls over with sudden urgency when she sees a giant puffball or flowers on the roadside; she and her siblings are sent into the hedgerow to gather precious treasures. They are sometimes late to arrive on account of passing flora and fungi. When their mother is in the caravan there are wildflowers and decorative weeds in vases and mugs.

The frying garlic is so fragrant it envelops us in a sweet, potent cloud. It is a lot for the morning – an adventure in garlic. The scent becomes richer as she adds roughly chopped mushrooms and then parsley, which is more fragrant still. The kitchen area in the caravan is small and dark as the light is shaded out by trees, but the low lighting only adds to the sense of magic. Tired from a late night gossiping in the tent, I sit on the oat-coloured sofa that runs round the wall of the caravan's living-room area with the two sisters and their two brothers and their father. We wait for mushrooms and pieces of bread, eyeing plates jealously as they emerge from the kitchen to make sure no one has more than us. We exclaim *how delicious* and really mean it. After breakfast, my friends' mum sits on the steps into the caravan to smoke a cigarette and drinks strong, thick coffee.

The woods in which the caravans are situated are at the top of an earthy cliff that is made cool even in the hottest part of the day by hundreds of sycamores that grow like weeds on its steep slopes. Once the younger sister and I – my closest friend by the river – find a clearing in the woods with a single tree growing in it covered in pink flowers and glossy deep green leaves. We call it 'the rose tree' and sing to it and make it offerings that we bury at its base. At the bottom of the cliff, rhododendrons grow rampant, their huge clusters of purple flowers glowing in the dim light. One night we camp out in the hollow space at the centre of a rhododendron bush. We spend the day collecting washed-up planks from the shore of the river to make a 'floor' and bring sleeping bags down from the caravans. We are eaten alive by mosquitos and I stay awake most of the night listening keenly for animals.

Beyond the rhododendrons is a strip of sand, then an expanse of oily mud that is revealed at low tide, then the river with moored boats and passing container ships ferrying goods up and down stream. Sometimes men walk out into the thick mud up to their knees to gather bait for fishing – fanged ragworms that live in the mud. On the strip of sand on the shoreline, we make a fire and cook 'dampers', a thrilling foodstuff introduced by my friends' mum. We make a dough by mixing water and flour and shape a small ball of it onto the end of sticks from the trees that surround us. We hold the sticks over the fire to cook the dough, rotating them to make sure it cooks evenly, and when it's scorched and smells a little like bread, we remove the dough and fill the hole left by the stick with butter or jam.

Sometimes I am nervous about trying the unfamiliar dishes made by my friends' mother – she tests my openness to new things. On another occasion I watch her scramble eggs with fresh tomatoes and herbs in a pan – I have not seen eggs prepared like this and I am hesitant about egg-eating. A decade later when I love eggs, I repeat her gestures with egg and tomato and find I love eggs and tomatoes together very much. Each time I see her cook, she prepares ingredients in ways I have not encountered before, extending my understanding of what is possible. Once while making dinner, she has the idea to take a small log from the fire and put it in the oven for a few minutes to introduce smokiness to a shoulder of lamb. Her unaffected openness in the kitchen extends to other areas of embodiment, too. She is the first woman I know who does not shave her armpits or wear a bra, and she loves to wear little strappy tops in which both facts are visible; as a child I reflect on this often. She remains the only person I know who exhibits such freedom with her body until I go to nightclubs in the city in my late teens. It was her idea to pitch the tent and even when it's her last few quid, she gives it to us to buy ice-cream.

River Mumma

NIELLAH ARBOINE

She sits perched on a large grey rock on the river's bank, humming a tune older than the trees. In her left hand she holds a golden comb, and using her right, she grabs sections of hair and pulls the blunt teeth through her strands, starting at the top of her damp head and working her way to the tips. She begins the process again, methodically.

Her eyes, black as the shiny seeds of ackee fruit, flutter open below curly lashes. As she adjusts her position, her thick tail slithers along with her, the slick-wet iridescence of scales turning dull as they dry under dusk's fleeting light.

Today she inspects the head of a young bull propped up on a rock. The offering is still warm to the touch, and the metallic smell of blood smudges the air. She pries open his mouth and runs her webbed fingers across his lower teeth, then looks deeply into his glassy eyes. Next, she dips her tongue into the pool of sticky blood congealing at the stump of his neck. Satisfied, she scoops up the bull's head, then plunges back into the cool lizard-green water.

That evening, she watches lines of tired, sore feet trudge across the width of the river bed, clambering over boulders. They whisper thanks to her. River Mumma lets them pass this time.

When my mum was pregnant with me, she knew I would be named after the longest river in the world. If I had been a boy, I would have been called Nile, but I wasn't and so, with some imagination, she came up with Niellah.

There is something in naming; it sets out intentions for you long before you might know or live up to them; I have always been a child of water. For as long as I can remember, I have felt a deep affinity with oceans, lakes and especially rivers. I've never feared water and its vastness, nor have I found its endless rhythms daunting. Water is complicated to the diaspora I belong to – it carries pain, freedom, fear, death, rebirth and salvation. To me it feels cleansing, soothing, even hypnotising, like meeting a forgotten part of myself, like reconnecting to who I am, where I come from, and where I'll eventually return.

I think of all the rivers I've encountered so far, and how many of them are flecked with memories of my happiest moments. The Ardèche, the Hase, the Cherwell, the Severn, the Douro, the Iguazu and even the Thames. But of all the rivers of my life, I cling most dearly to those in Jamaica.

Jamaica was named by the Indigenous Taíno people – Xaymaca – meaning 'land of wood and water'. Not only is it an island surrounded by water, it homes around 120 rivers, running through almost every parish.

Castleton Botanical Gardens, founded in 1862, is one of the oldest botanical gardens in the Caribbean with over 250 major plant species. It sits in a mountain valley at the bank of Wag Water River, which meanders through Castleton in the parish of St Mary. This river is particularly special to my family. Locals and tourists have been coming to Castleton Gardens for generations to relax, swim and bask in all its natural beauty.

My grandma would often visit Wag Water in her youth, before she left for Britain to train as a nurse. As I ask her about rivers on a recent trip to visit her in Jamaica, she furrows her brow while reaching back into her mind to conjure up the past. She tells me tales about walking for miles with school or church friends to Castleton Gardens on the weekends. Some folks would swim, others would paddle, and those who couldn't swim would settle on boulders while the rest cooked along the river's edge. During storms, my grandma would place branches across the local stream to stop fruit and vegetables – coconuts, breadfruits – from being carried downstream.

When my older brother and I stayed with her over long summers as children, she'd take us to the same river over and over again. We stayed high up in the peaks of Jamaica, with the blue mountains on the horizon, far from the bleached white beaches of tourist postcards. Here, the closest bodies of water are rivers and streams curling down from the hills, eventually meeting the sea. We'd spend the whole day in Castleton Gardens, splashing in the water, jumping off rocks and squealing into the warm breeze while grandma sat watching, in the shade of a tree on the river's bank.

I recently returned to Castleton after an eighteen-year gap; the river still remembered me. This time, my younger brother and I watched shoals of silver fish swirl around our legs and lemon-yellow butterflies spiral above our heads, while our mum sat watching from the river's bank, just as my grandma did all those years ago. We let the force of the water wash our bodies down the river's many cascades, before spitting us into the gurgling fizz of white below. We perched on boulders and sunned our shoulders while gazing up at the valley's towering wall of green vines and trees. We clambered up the same rock faces I had jumped off as a child, back when I didn't fear falling or flying. I thought about how much I'd changed since I had last swum in these waters and how, in many ways, the river hadn't – or had it? While I'd grown in stature, it felt as though the river might have shrunk. In those moments, my brother and I decided we saw God here more than we did between any four walls. I remember who I am when I'm in those familiar waters.

But this river carries much more than our happy memories; according to Jamaican folklore, it also homes River Mumma.

Merpeople and water spirits appear in folklore across the globe, in countless cultures. Given most of the Earth's surface consists of water, it feels only natural to question the multitude of worlds beneath this exterior. From Mami Wata in African and diasporic folklores, Hai Ho Shang in China – a merman with the body of a fish and the head of a Buddhist monk – to the Nibiinaabe, a race of water spirits from the Indigenous Ojibwe people, hailing from present-day Canada and the north of the United States, and Rusalka, a water spirit from Slavic countries, merfolk have captivated the human imagination, swimming through our collective consciousness.

Tales of mermaids and water spirits fill the rivers and seas of the Caribbean: Mami Wata and Oshun swam alongside enslaved Africans on their forced passage to other worlds, holding those who were lost to the sea, and guiding those who remained. I imagine these water spirits and deities, as well as the selkies from Irish shores, accumulated and formed the ancient River Mumma in the minds of many.

While visiting Jamaica around Christmas one year, my brothers, mum and I all sat in my grandma's living room with her and a few family friends from the neighbourhood, the door left ajar and the white grate closed, as rain pattered on the flat roof. I asked what they all knew about mermaids, assuming I'd be told that they were the stuff of legend, or cautionary stories. But instead, everyone talked about River Mumma in the same way one would talk about the weather – a fact of daily life. While Jamaica is a reasonably conservative society, superstitions and an unwavering belief in the supernatural have always permeated the nation with traditions, stories and mythologies, surviving slavery into the present day. And the belief in River Mumma is no exception. Both feared and revered, she can protect and provide or drown and seek vengeance just as quickly. It is believed that enslaved people would make sacrifices, such as bulls' heads, to River Mumma for safe passage across her waters, and in times of drought, they would call upon her to bring them water.

Unlike most merpeople, River Mumma does not live in the sea. She resides in snaking rivers with fresh-water fish as children. In some anecdotes, the name River Mumma is used as a general umbrella term for mermaids who are spotted in multiple locations in Jamaica, including in dreams. According to others, though, all these stories and legends are the workings of one mermaid.

River Mumma, I am told, is fond of blood sacrifices, as well as sacrificial bulls' heads. She also has a keen eye for gold. She has been spotted sitting on rocks, combing her dark hair with the golden comb she loves so dearly. It is said that there is even a gold table in her lair, left behind by Spanish colonisers, which she now fiercely protects.

More than anything, River Mumma is powerful, hypnotic and dangerous, sometimes even visiting people in their dreams and tempting them. In one story, near Coakley in the parish my family hails from, River

Mumma's golden table was seen rising out of the water. One day, a local man decided to use his donkeys and mules to drag the table out of the river with a rope. But as they pulled and pulled, the table began to sink, dragging down the animals and almost drowning the local man himself.

Decades ago in Wag Water, the same river I'd swum in with my brothers, the beloved pastor of my grandma's church was baptising parish members when he felt River Mumma's pull. He could not see her but he could sense her presence and immediately knew River Mumma lurked in the waters beneath. He tried to get himself out of the river, but her grip was too strong, dragging him back from the bank. It was only when he reached into his pocket and pulled out a handkerchief, quickly tied a knot in it and threw it into the water, that he was released from her embrace.

There is one place in Jamaica where her might is felt the most: the Bog Walk gorge in the parish of St Catherine. Southeast of the island, the Rio Cobre flows under Flat Bridge. If you ask a Jamaican about Flat Bridge, they will tell you about mermaids. Countless curious incidents have occurred around this bridge, and some locals believe that these can only be explained by the hauntings of a mermaid.

Flat Bridge is one of the oldest bridges in Jamaica, constructed by Spanish colonisers around four centuries ago and built by enslaved Africans from sixteen different plantations. Vehicles have mysteriously plummeted off the beam bridge and into the depths of the river below, killing numerous people over the years. This could be chalked down to tragic accidents due to dangerous driving, the bridge's lack of railings, or strong currents dragging people away. But many have concluded that the bridge is haunted and these deaths are the work of a mermaid, and her need for a blood sacrifice. She is said to appear when the river turns lizard-green; this is when River Mumma's power reaches its peak, causing those nearby to lose consciousness and topple into the water.

I find myself wondering: why doesn't a bridge that has taken so many lives have barriers? Well, it has been said that every time fencing is erected, it is all too soon destroyed by the elements and sucked into the river. Again: the chilling actions of a mermaid?

After all these stories, it is difficult not to believe in the power of River Mumma; if not as a physical being, then certainly as a force created from the depths of history, fear, creativity and the faith of a people. Stories of River Mumma have survived voyages, colonisation and even death itself. To know her is to know the resistance of a people.

I wonder how long River Mumma will live in these rivers. Can you kill a spirit?

Sometimes I think about the streams and rivers drying up once we've taken everything River Mumma has known and respected, leaving nothing behind but sticky clay and exposed rock, bleached by the sun. I think about how Wag Water River seemed shallower when I visited last year, and whether this would be its new path. Maybe River Mumma will also shrink and shrink until she is the size of a smooth pebble.

I think of her choking on toxic chemicals dribbling down into her home. Would this sting and blur her vision? I think about her ingesting foreign microplastics, crystallising her from the inside out. I think about how the world's freshwater species have been rapidly declining over the last five decades, and I imagine River Mumma looking on helplessly while her children suffocate. How would it feel to watch her children dying overnight, her grief sharp and sudden?

River Mumma wonders why she ever bothered helping us or visiting at all. How could these land walkers be so cruel, so selfish? Why do they try and fight against the current? How strange it must be to have lived for centuries, then to suddenly have everything you hold dear ripped away from you.

Sometimes, I think of River Mumma's vengeful tears flooding the river, bursting through banks and breaking down dams, submerging the land and claiming more blood than she could possibly know what to do with. I think of her becoming engorged, growing larger than any river could hold. Spilling down the delta and into the sea, salt stinging her wounds and eyes.

Will she forget us? I know that, whatever happens, River Mumma will continue humming her songs long after we're gone.

Crossing the River

Approaching the Itchen

ROGER DEAKIN

Approaching the Itchen along College Walk, I came eventually to the water meadows and two or three piebald horses grazing by the river. I vaulted a low fence, steadying myself on a PRIVATE FISHING notice, and crossed the meadow to a convenient willow, where I changed into bathing trunks and a pair of wetsuit boots for the return journey from my swim, and sank my rucksack and clothes into a patch of nettles. At the chalky, gravel bank I confirmed Cobbett's observation, made on 9 November 1822, that: 'The water in the Itchen is, they say, *famed* for its *clearness*.' I plunged into the river, which was three to four feet deep, with here and there a shallow, sandy bank cushioned by water crowfoot. The current was fast enough to make it slow going if I turned and struck out upstream. But I rode downstream with the river in a leisurely breaststroke, keeping my eyes open for whatever might be round the next bend. I was rewarded with the sight of a water vole crossing over and disappearing into the reed-bed on the far bank. The river swung round in a long arc through the water meadows, and very sweet it was too. Here and there I saw the dark forms of trout, and minnows hung in the sandy riffles. This was very fine swimming, and I continued downstream towards the places once known as Milkhole and Dalmatia, where the Winchester College boys used to swim. The Itchen is fed at intervals by natural springs, which is why there are watercress beds along the valley. At Gunner's Hole, a fabled bathing pool further upstream which I intended to explore in due course, the springs are said to create dangerous undercurrents from time to time, and in the early part of this century a boy was drowned there. What the college now calls 'proper swimming' only began in 1969 when an indoor pool was built.

Breaststroking softly through this famously clear water I was soon dreaming of the strawberry garden at the family seat of the Ogles at Martyr Worthy upstream, thus described by Cobbett:

> A beautiful strawberry garden, capable of being watered by a branch of the Itchen which comes close by it, and

which is, I suppose, brought there on purpose. Just by, on the greensward, under the shade of very fine trees, is an alcove, wherein to sit to eat the strawberries, coming from the little garden just mentioned, and met by bowls of cream coming from a little milk-house, shaded by another clump a little lower down the stream. What delight! What a terrestrial paradise!

I had climbed out of the river and was strolling back through the lovely water meadows still far away in my daydream, milkmaids plying me with laden bowls of fresh strawberries and cream, when a *shout* rudely intruded on my pink and brown study: 'Do you realise this is private property?' The horses looked up for a moment and resumed their grazing. I decided to ignore the two irate figures on the fenced foot-path and pressed on with all dignity in my bathing trunks towards the hidden clothes in the nettle patch. It crossed my mind to make my escape across the water, but then I thought of Cobbett and what he would have done, and that settled it. I was going to stand up for my rights as a free swimmer.

I got changed as languidly as possible, then casually leapfrogged the fence and sauntered off along the path, whistling softly to myself, as an Englishman is entitled to do. 'Excuse me,' came a voice, 'does that fence mean anything to you?' This was unmistakable school talk, and I turned round to confront two figures straight out of Dickens; a short and portly porter with a beard and Alsatian, and a gangling figure on a bike with binoculars, strawberry-pink with ire, the College River Keeper. I introduced myself and enquired the cause of their disquiet. They said the river was the property of the college, and full of trout for the pleasure of the Old Wykehamists who sometimes fish there. It was definitely not for swimming in by *hoi polloi*.

'But the ladies in the public library told me the whole of Winchester used to swim in the river here right up to the 1970s,' I said.

'That's just the problem,' they replied. 'A few years ago we had six hundred people coming from the town, swimming in the river, eroding the banks and leaving litter behind.'

It sounded like paradise to me.

'But surely,' I said sweetly, 'we should all have access to swim in our rivers just as we should be free to walk in our own countryside. Don't they belong to all of us?'

The River Keeper practically fell off his bike. The porter flushed a deeper strawberry and allowed the Alsatian a little closer to my person. They both looked pityingly at me.

'There's plenty of coast and sea not far away if you want to swim,' ventured the porter.

At this point things suddenly turned nasty. They accused me of scaring away the trout and the porter muttered about calling the police. I said stoutly, and perhaps unwisely, that if I frightened away the fish, which I doubted, perhaps I was doing them a good turn, since if they stayed they would only be murdered by the Old Wykehamists. I told them I swim in the Waveney all the time in Suffolk in a place where bathers and anglers have co-existed happily for at least a century. And anyway, I said, why not designate one stretch of river for bathing and another for the Old Wykehamist fly-fishermen?

'We couldn't possibly do that because the water quality is too dodgy,' said the porter. 'Upstream of here they spray pesticides on the watercress beds and there's a sewage works discharging what should be clean water, but isn't always, into the river.'

I quoted Cobbett to them on the famously clear water. They laughed. There was no sign of the police, but the porter urged me to go away immediately and have a shower with plenty of hot water and soap to wash off all the pollutants in the river. People had been getting skin rashes, he said. Wishful thinking on his part, I fancied.

'But if the water is so evil and polluted, why aren't the trout all dead?' I asked. 'And why have you fenced in this footpath in a straight line miles away from the river instead of letting people enjoy winding along the lovely banks? Isn't that a bit mean?'

'I'm not wasting any more time with this,' he said, and flounced off, the Alsatian casting hungry looks over its shoulder.

The episode raised some serious issues about swimming in the wild, if you can call Winchester wild. I reflected again on Cobbett, and how upset he was at the hanging of two men in Winchester in the spring of 1822 for resisting the gamekeepers of Mr Assheton-Smith at nearby Tidworth. What they did amounted to little more than I had just done, yet I had not, in the end, been marched, dripping, up the hill to join Grobbelaar and Co. in the dock. Things were changing in Winchester, but only slowly. The truth was, I had enjoyed my row with the water bailiffs very much. I already felt invigorated after a really first-class swim, and now I felt even better after a terrific set-to. But it seemed sad, and a real loss to the city, that the college no longer allowed swimmers in the river, or picnickers on the water meadows. I was left feeling very much like the otter, 'trapped but not detained', by one of the Houghton Club keepers in December 1853.

The matter of ownership of a river is fairly simple. Where a river runs through private land, the riparian owner also owns the river itself. On the question of access, the key legislation is the 1968 Countryside Act, which deliberately defined riverside and woodland as 'open country' in addition to the 'mountain, moor, heathland, cliff, downland and foreshore' originally listed in the 1949 National Parks and Access to the Countryside Act. 'Riverside' includes the river as well as the banks in the definition of the Act. So whenever politicians mention 'open country' they are talking about rivers and their banks, as well as all those other kinds of countryside such as mountains and moorland. And when the Labour Party Policy Commission on the Environment promised, in July 1994, 'Labour's commitment to the environment will be backed up with legally enforceable environmental rights: a right of access to common land, open country, mountain and moorland,' they meant rivers and riverbanks too.

On the very same day as my Winchester fracas, Chris Smith, the Secretary of State for National Heritage, had been saying: 'I look forward, as Heritage Secretary, to working in partnership with the Ramblers' Association to secure access to open country, mountain and moorland for the ordinary people of Britain. Let's make a "right to roam" a reality!' So how about the right to swim? That so many of our rivers should be inaccessible to all but a tiny minority who can afford to pay for fishing 'rights' is surely unjust? I say 'rights' to point up the paradox, that something that *was* once a natural right has been expropriated and turned into a commodity. Fishing rights are only valuable because individuals have eliminated a public benefit – access to their rivers – to create an artificial private gain. The right to walk freely along riverbanks or to bathe in rivers, should no more be bought and sold than the right to walk up mountains or to swim in the sea from our beaches. At the moment, only where a river is navigable do you have rights of access along its banks.

In a recent survey of public opinion, the Countryside Commission discovered that one in three of all the walks people take in Britain involves water, or waterside, as a valued feature. In April 1967, a government official drawing up the 1968 Countryside Act observed:

> We have received a considerable volume of representations that the present arrangements for securing public access and providing a right of public passage on waterways is inadequate. In our opinion the solution lies in extending the powers to make access agreements or orders to rivers and canals and their banks ... and we would propose therefore to extend the definition of open country to include these categories.

The flaw in the 1968 Countryside Act turned out to be that it relied on giving local authorities powers, but not *duties*, to create more access to rivers and their banks. Making voluntary agreements with private landowners could still work, if only the local authorities put more energy into it, and if only the landowners didn't have such enormous vested interest in the lucrative fishery. The government now says it will 'seek more access by voluntary means to riverside, woodland and other countryside as appropriate'. There is plenty of scope for such schemes: if all the riverbanks in Buckinghamshire were opened for public access, it would double the total length of footpaths in that county. Riverside access is extremely popular. Perhaps we should learn from New Zealand, where they have renewed a law originally enacted by a colonial governor at the request of Queen Victoria. 'The Queen's Chain' gives a twenty-two-yard strip of public access along the bank of every river in the land. Across the Channel in Normandy and Brittany, too, people have unlimited access to the rivers.

The Environment Agency, meanwhile, is being influenced by the powerful vested interests of the riparian owners into confusing the natural value of chalk rivers like the Itchen and the Test with their commercial value. It is allowing them to be managed exclusively for the benefit of trout fishery along much of their length. What were once richly varied wild trout rivers have been allowed to become highly manipulated leisure enterprises capable of delivering a more or less guaranteed catch of four or five fish to the people, often tourists, who can pay to fish there. Trout fisheries also persecute the pike, culling coarse fish by electro-fishing, even removing such essentials to the ecology of natural chalk streams as brook lampreys and bullheads. Besides all this, they cut and remove the weed that would otherwise naturally hold up the flow and maintain the depth of water, as well as harbouring the invertebrates that provide vital food in the rivers' ecosystems. On one short stretch of the Test above Whitchurch, the owner deploys over sixty different traps for stoats and weasels along the banks, which tend to be manicured of their natural cover with strimmers to accommodate the fastidious new breed of angler. What is at stake is the very resource that, left alone, would create and sustain the wild trout: the natural chalk stream.

Crayfish were once so abundant in the Itchen that when the river keepers cleared gratings and sluices along Winchester College water meadows, there would be dozens of them amongst the weed. But a few years ago the fish farms upstream introduced the American crayfish. The new arrivals carried a fatal disease, the crayfish plague, to which they, but not our native species, had developed immunity. The result has been the near-extinction of the wild crayfish from the Itchen. They are now reduced to a few isolated populations in side-streams or backwaters, having been replaced by their American cousins.

Now that the coast was clear again, I sauntered along the footpath across St Stephen's Mead, in search of the once popular college bathing hole, Gunner's Hole. It was called after the Rev. H. Gunner, one of the college chaplains. There used to be a wide arc of changing sheds following the curve of the riverbank, thatched huts on an island, and a system of sluices to regulate the natural flow of the water. Gunner's Hole was about a hundred yards long and twelve yards wide, and the stretch of river was dredged of mud and concreted along its banks towards the end of the nineteenth century. It even had a handrail around the area of 'a high diving erection with four stages and two spring-boards', as the *Public Schools' Handbook* called it in 1900, continuing enthusiastically: 'Gunner's Hole is now second to none as a bathing place in England. Here, under the shade of the limes, are the best features of a swimming bath and a river rolled into one.'

Sure enough, Gunner's Hole was still there, secluded under the shade of enormous plane trees and poplars, one or two now tumbled over the water. Its motion-less surface was entirely covered by a classic duckweed lawn, the fabled disguise of Creeping Jenny, a monster of nursery folklore who would suck children under if they went too close, closing innocently over them to hide all trace of their fate. The massive concrete walls of the pool were in surprisingly good condition, and, on the basis that stolen fruit always tastes sweetest, I climbed through the concrete river inlet sluice to drop in silently at the deep end. Sinking through the opaque green cloak was like breaking the ice. I laboured down the hundred yards of the pool, mowing a path in the lawn which closed behind me as I went. Moorhens scampered off, half-flying over the billiard-baize green. The water beneath was still deep, but no longer the ten feet it used to be below the diving boards. It had silted up to between five and seven feet. Reaching down, I felt soft mud and ancient fallen branches, and sensed giant pike and eels.

Breaststroking back like a fly in soup, I reflected that Gunner's Hole must have been where one of the legendary sea-swimmers of our times evolved his style. Sir James Lighthill was amongst the great mathematical scientists of the century. He became Lucasian Professor of Mathematics at Cambridge, and later Provost of University College, London. From Winchester he won a scholarship to Trinity College, Cambridge at the age of fifteen, and became a fellow at twenty-one. Lighthill was pre-eminent in the field of wave theory and fluid dynamics, and studied and analysed the pattern of the fierce currents that run round the Channel Islands. He was a strong swimmer, and put his knowledge to the test by becoming one of the first to swim the eighteen miles round Sark in 1973. By careful homework,

Lighthill calculated the best course and timing to take advantage of the swirling, ferocious tides and currents. In ensuing years he returned and swam round the island five times. On his sixth island tour, in July 1998, aged seventy-four, he swam all day and was close to completing his nine-hour voyage when he ran into some rough seas. He was seen to stop swimming and died close to the shore. As was his custom, he was alone and had no boat with him. He regarded swimming as 'a most pleasant way to see the scenery', and swam on his back to conserve energy, describing his style as 'a two-arm, two-leg backstroke, thrusting with the arms and legs alternately'. I imagined the young Lighthill swimming up and down Gunner's Hole on summer evenings, perfecting his stroke, observing the complexities of the swimming style of the stickleback, and calculating distances.

There was no longer any sign of the diving boards or the changing sheds, still marked on the 1953 Ordnance Survey map, but when I swam back to the concrete inlet I caught hold of a bit of the original handrail and climbed over into the fresh, fast water of the main river. In a metaphor for its history, Gunner's Hole used to carry the main stream, and is now a backwater. Dropping into a pool above the main sluice that controls the river level, I shed duckweed in a green confetti ribbon that went licking away on the stream.

Standing chest deep, pinioned to the slippery wooden sluice gates whose grain stood out like corduroy, I imagined a future without fish farms or watercress beds, when the river could flow as sweetly as ever it did in Cobbett's day, and there could be bathing again in Gunner's Hole.

What is a River?

AMY-JANE BEER

Something happens to our brains when we stare at moving water: a sort of broad, effortless attentiveness, the effects of which are regarded as restorative and pleasurable. Psychologists call this state 'soft fascination' and suggest that in it we might find relief from anxiety and mental fatigue, and open our minds to free-wheeling patterns of thought. Spend a quiet hour on a riverbank watching water slide by and you might find yourself wondering where it comes from, and where it might be going. You might even ask yourself *What is a river?* The answer is simultaneously simple enough that it is taught to nursery age children, and vast and complex enough that the mind struggles to hold it all. If from your seat on the bank you chose to follow that water in your mind, on to its destination, or back to its source, you find yourself on a never-ending spiral through time and space. A river is not the bounded thing it might first appear it to be.

To me, for many years, rivers meant adventure, challenge, adrenaline. The kayaking years, when almost every weekend and almost every holiday would see us loading boats onto cars, sometimes onto planes, and even a few times strapping them to helicopters, and chasing rain or melt. There's not much to match white water paddling for physical, emotional and technical challenges or opportunities to experience places and sights most people rarely get to see. Mountaineers, cavers, divers, sky divers and off-piste skiers understand – and I tried all those things too, but for me, the sheer wildness of the ride and the sensation of being simultaneously carried by and part of the flow made kayaking hard to match. Then, in 2012, the joy and the thrill became awful, heart-shattering loss. That of Kate, a beloved friend, a wife, a mother, a daughter, a sister, an extraordinary person. She was a highly competent paddler, running a river as part of a well-skilled team. But flow can be chaotic, and sometimes it takes even the best. It was almost seven years before I could bring myself to visit the place. Years in which I grew older, more cautious, a mother myself. But when I did go there, I found something I wasn't expecting. Not

closure, or peace, or even the words to say goodbye . . .
none of the things I was probably looking for. Instead
I found wonder and a sort of gentle tug, as familiar and
insistent as gravity.

In the space below the ferocious pot-bellied rapid
that held Kate just out of reach for ten minutes, there
is a pool of calm water. And in crouching by that pool
I saw a feature of flow so delicate I'd never noticed one
before. At first, I thought it was a thread of spider silk
or discarded fishing line floating on the surface. But
after watching more closely I realised it was a boundary,
hanging vertically like a veil in the water from the
surface to the depths, visible only as a slight perturba-
tion of light. It had no substance. It disappeared when
I touched it and reformed when I took my fingers
away. It dawned on me that what I was seeing was
an interface between opposing flows – an eddyline. It
was like seeing the join between past and present, life
and death – the tiniest nothing between enormities.
The longer I watched, the more other subtle features I
saw: tiny boils and upwellings and vortices that created
small dimples in the surface, as though someone had
touched the water and it remembered. It made me
wonder what else I might have missed in all the years
of chasing rainbows and adventure, and I decided it
was time to go back, only more slowly and much more
attentively than before.

I returned to that same spot a few months later, on the first of January, seven years to the day after Kate's accident, and I stripped naked and swam. I don't remember being baptised – it wasn't something I had a choice or active part in, but it's clear to anyone familiar with the buzz of cold water why immersion might be incorporated into ritual rites. In a part of my brain long forgotten until that icy swim, aquatic ancestors stirred in their sleep. I woke up.

What is a river? Three years later, I've found many answers. So many it's hard to hold them all. None are new. People have been making watery journeys of physical, intellectual, emotional and spiritual discovery forever. Asking old questions encourages you to consider old ways of thinking alongside the new.

In its durability and abundance, water reveals how small our lives are in time as well as space. Less than 0.025 per cent of water on our planet exists at any one time in all the world's rivers, lakes, marshes and biological organisms combined. A river is water's very occasional chance to flicker and dance under the sun before it returns to the deep, dark ocean, is frozen in ice or stored away underground, sometimes for hundreds of millennia at a stretch. Flowing water moves mountains, it hollows and builds land. It provides the medium in which the chemistry of life recycles and reorganises energy and matter. There's a river running through you, now. Tomorrow its substance will be somewhere else and you'll be imbibing more of the stuff of oceans and glaciers, of sweat and spit, of blood and sap, of bog and mud and pee, of vapour and clouds and rain and snow. It's all river, all flow.

What is a river? Rivers are life, health, history, story, reflection, transmission, awe. They can be barriers and obstacles and boundaries, but more often they are corridors, portals, thin places or confluences. Like water itself, a river can be a giver and taker of life. This duality and the tendency of water to change state from ice to liquid to vapour, runs thick in mythologies and theologies from around the world. The avatars of rivers include a host of deities, spirits, monsters and imaginary beings, and most are halflings, chimeras or shapeshifters, offering sex and death, beauty and horror, fecundity and obliteration, kindness and ferocity. Myths often spiral in a manner very similar to the water cycle, revisiting themes or places similar to those they have been before, taking the form from their surroundings. We are transfixed and beguiled by the parts we can see, while the rest is like water in deep storage: we know it is there, but we can't reach it.

The biological denizens of rivers give us stories every bit as weird and wonderful. These include cautionary tales and reasons for hope and unrivalled metaphors for resilience and change: the hero's journey of salmon,

the vigour of willows, the defibrillating shock of king-
fisher flight, the dipper whose song carries clear over
the rush of water, the transformations and ascension
of the mayfly. These species have become my familiars,
my totems and my guides.

I didn't set out to write a pandemic book. But the
pandemic happened, and the experience of alternating
lockdown and release, not to mention the existential
anxiety visited on us all undoubtedly channelled my
thoughts. The first few excursions after months at
home had an almost unravelling effect. In the run up
to the autumn equinox in September 2020 I took a
trip to Wales. Unseasonal heat, clear and starry night
skies, and long hours of unaccustomed solitude sent
my imagination on a rampage. My dreams were wild.
On the banks of the Severn, late at night, the new
moon tugged, and brought a monster upstream – a
tidal bore, the river devouring itself. On a steep and
tiny tributary of the Afon Dyfi, an old, old story of
transformation told by a collector of river songs called
me to embrace change while remaining true to myself;
and an experience of snorkelling in a narrow canyon
where salmon and sea trout come to spawn showed
me something of how to do that. These are fish which
change their skins and their physiology to move as
they must between fresh and salt, but never forget their
origins, and change again when the time comes to

return. And in that uphill struggle, with odds against them, they seek allowances, using eddies and recirculation created by the very flow that threatens to push them back, biding their time, and in doing so they achieve what sometimes seems impossible.

That Welsh gorge, with its extraordinary underwater rock formations lit with cathedral light, golden and aquamarine, was as good a place as any for a religious moment. Only it wasn't a god that I found, so much as a sense of indigeneity. A military brat from birth, my early childhood was happy, secure, but geographically rootless, lived on tours of duty in places that weren't home. I was a child of my parents and of the British Army, born in Germany, but not *from* anywhere. In place of roots there were flags and anthems, and the rules of cricket and Enid Blyton ideas of decency. I guess that was good enough then, but in recent years, I'd become uneasy with almost every aspect of my nationality and begun seeking a different kind of belonging. In a matrix created by myths, by constellations, by the taste of water flowing from a specific geology, by human and non-human ancestors, by species and communities of life we share the land and the water with, I've found the coordinates for a place that feels like home, and I love it more than I could ever love a flag flying over the land or an individual presiding over it. The folk singer and song collector Owen Shiers uses the word *cynefin* to describe this niche within a web of culture and nature, and the idea has thrown me a line I never knew I needed.

The power of indigenous thinking is being belatedly acknowledged, or should I say rediscovered, by the developed world in the battle for climate justice, in land rights, in conservation. In one of many examples, the Maori concept of kaitiakitanga calls on individuals, communities and societies to recognise the complex interconnected nature of the human and non-human world and act to safeguard species and ecologies, landscapes and waters, languages and culture. How extraordinary that for all the depth and breadth, diversity and specificity of the English language, we have no words for cynefin or kaitiakitanga. The lack means we are suffering an unnamed loss: a recent survey[1] ranked the UK lowest of fourteen European countries in nature connectedness. The pandemic gave me a new insight into what this collective nature deficit might mean. During lockdown, our local river, the Yorkshire Derwent, was a godsend. In easy walking distance, I swam there often, feeling indescribable relief that it was possible, but also guilt, not for the technical trespass of entering water on land I don't own, but that this simple restorative therapy was something denied to so many. That awareness has stayed with me as COVID restrictions have eased, because millions of people still live without free access to wild green and blue space close to where they live.

What is a river? There are other ways of addressing the question, and other reasons for asking it. In 1991, in the denouement of a seven-year legal battle over navigation rights on this very river, the question was given a legal framing and asked of the most senior court in the land, the House of Lords. Their verdict, that a river was . . . a river, had profound implications. Under the Rights of Way Act of 1932, a Public Right of Way can be established across land if it has been used as such for a period of twenty years, and this includes 'land covered by water'. The Lords' ruling meant that laws dealing with land and specifically with rights of way over it, cannot be applied to flowing water.

It is unfortunate that this particular battle was fought between developers wanting to profit from the building of marinas and infrastructure on the Derwent and riparian landowners who by and large don't want to share it. It was reduced to a binary matter: the right to exploit versus the right to exclude, decided on the basis of property law. Both sides rallied groups who loved and understood the river in different ways – anglers and conservationists sided with the landowners to prevent development, pleasure boaters and heritage enthusiasts wanting to see restoration of locks and other infrastructure took the developers' side.

As a paddler and an environmentalist, I despair at the failure of the law to recognise nuance. As so often happens when complex issues are reduced to binaries, the majority are left stranded. A canoe is no threat to the river and yet that case means that for most of the length of the Derwent there is no automatic right of navigation for any craft, be it a cargo barge, a party-cruiser or a coracle. While this case was unusual in having been handed down from such a senior court, the exclusion it brought is the norm across England, where the public has a statutory right of access to a mere three per cent of rivers. In the other ninety-seven per cent if you swim or float along in any kind of watercraft, you're likely to be committing trespass, thanks to nonsensical law that equates your existence in that spot with harm to the landowner, regardless of whether any actual harm is caused. Even the opportunity to sit peacefully on the bank is often limited to those privileged by wealth or circumstance, or willing to trespass for it. In England, access to rivers is even more limited than our access to land, of which we have freedom to roam over around 8%. And yes I know all about our network of public rights of way, some of which follow rivers. But a right of way is for moving along. It is not a right to sit and stare. This legal absurdity means that many of the activists at the forefront of campaigns to protect and restore our rivers, including swimmers, paddlers, anglers and naturalists, must routinely trespass in order to access the water. While statutory bodies fail dismally to regulate or protect, tiny grassroots organisations and lone individuals are punching far above their weight in highlighting sewage and agricultural slurry pollution, over-abstraction from chalk rivers and the ubiquity of microplastics. They are clearing litter, monitoring species and tackling the spread of non-native invasives. Interestingly, these actions are very much in keeping with the responsibilities of kaitiakitanga. So are the actions of some local communities following legal precedents in other nations by declaring rights of nature, starting in 2021 with a group dedicated to the rights of Cambridge's eponymous River Cam. Perhaps we can make amends after all.

I'm not the woman I was when I started writing my book, *The Flow*. It wasn't so much the rivers or the writing of them that changed me, but the attention-giving that doing so has required. We all change. It's easy to look back and see that, but also easy to forget that we remain a work in progress, and that like the many instars of a mayfly our future selves continue growing inside us until the day we die. In following the paths of water and asking old questions, I've seen those new stages emerge. I've found wonder and connection and a sense of my place, but also a call to act. I've discovered that I can't be a bystander.

What is a river? If you ask me now, I'd say it is a path. Whether you follow up or down, forward or backwards, doesn't matter. It's a circle you might never complete, but if you keep going long enough you'll be back somewhere close to where you began. What I can't say is what you might find on the way, or who you might be when you return.

Nightfishing

MICHAEL MALAY

The River Severn gleams under the moon, heavy with water, polished by light. Mist rolls from bank to bank, and the ground is firm and crisp, still hard from that year's winter. In the fields beyond the river, stray cattle pass like ghosts, and frost begins to form on the grass. It is very dark and very quiet.

The man next to me kneels down, tears a handful of grass and tosses it into the river. For a moment the grass spins, turns like a compass needle and then points southeast, towards the sea. The water carries it away. 'In ten minutes,' he says, 'the tide will turn and the grass will float back. That's when we put our nets in.' By the banks, where the willows gather, the water is dark. But at the river's centre, where the trees do not reach, the moon hammers down its brightness and there is a surfeit of glimmering light. 'They're coming,' he suddenly says, whether to me or to the river I'm not sure. 'I can feel it.'

We are there for eels. In particular, for the European eel, a creature known to science as *Anguilla anguilla*, but which anglers know by other names: fausen, gloat, gorb, scaffling, snig. The man's name is Andy and he has been fishing this river most of his life. The Sustainable Eel Group, which restocks rivers with the help of local anglers, put us in touch earlier that month. Andy's first email was to the point: 'Come up when the moon is full.'

And he is right: the eels are coming. Migrants of the high seas, they will have been travelling for years now, drifting along the highway of the Gulf Stream, across the freeway of the North Atlantic Drift, picking their way along ancient routes and water-paths, driven all the while by the promise of freshwater, safety, home. When they arrive, they will be thin and fragile, soft and tender, barely two years old. Yet they will already be veterans of the ocean, with three thousand miles under their belt. Their journey from the Sargasso Sea, a warm region of water in the north Atlantic, to the rivers and streams of Europe, is one of nature's headier miracles. That one eel arrives is astonishing. That millions of eels arrive each year defies belief.

I travelled from Bristol earlier that afternoon, taking a train to Gloucester before boarding a bus to Tirley, a small village eight miles north. The bus trundled down narrow roads of oak and lime, past fields of cowslip and dandelion, and everywhere you looked – in fields, ditches, alongside hedges – cow parsley was in flower, foaming white against the tender greens of early spring. After finding my accommodation for that night, a farmhouse that had been converted into a bed & breakfast, I went straight to sleep, though it was only 4 p.m. 'Get lots of rest,' Andy had texted earlier. 'You're going to need it.' When I next open my eyes, it is not to the familiar trees of my garden, birch and hawthorn, but to a paddock full of cows. House martins chatter under the eaves. The sun hangs low in the sky.

I turn on the radio. The news that day – the whole month, in fact – has been dominated by a political scandal. The Home Secretary has just resigned. Ministers have been called in for questioning. The Prime Minister's track record is being scrutinised. Across Britain, it appears that a systematic policy of detention and deportation has been in place, that citizens have been denied re-entry to their own country, that historic landing cards have been destroyed, jobs lost, and that men and women who were born here, or who emigrated here as children, have had their futures put in doubt, have been told that they are not British. Almost exclusively, those affected by these policies are people of colour, particularly members of the Windrush Generation and their children. Again and again, a quote is discussed on the radio – an excerpt from an interview given in 2012, 'The aim is to create, here in Britain, a really hostile environment for illegal immigrants.' The words of Theresa May, the country's former Home Secretary and, at the time of my visit to Tirley, the Prime Minister of the UK.

I turn off the radio and go outside. By the farm-house, a quiet lane takes me past stone cottages and thistly fields, before turning into a small track that leads into a woodland. A blackbird sings from an ash tree, and I listen as the last of the dusk slips away from the valley. Not long after returning to the farmhouse, another text comes through from Andy: 'Be ready for 10.30. And wear lots of warm clothes.'

We are standing on the banks, and Andy gives a low whistle, pointing to the river. A clump of grass floats by, followed by another. 'There,' he says, 'the tide has turned. The elvers will start running now.' We walk towards his car, near the small fire we have built by the bank, and he unfastens a net tied to the roof of his jeep. The net is huge – half a metre in width, a metre in length – and for a moment, as he lifts it, Andy looks incongruous, as though he were holding an oversize butterfly net. When we return to the river, he hammers two stakes into the ground, and then plunges the net into the water, scattering moonlight like phosphorescence. The net sits snugly on the bank, held in place by the two stakes. 'They're coming,' he says, for the second or third time that night. It's only his second week of fishing and he hasn't seen a single elver all spring, yet somehow he thinks tonight will be different, somehow he feels the eels will come.

It is. And they do. One hour past midnight, in a field deep in rural Gloucestershire, a net is lifted up, two faces peer down, and something precious is pulled up from the dark: an elver – frail, thin and milky-white. Andy transfers the creature into a bucket, and we pass the bucket from hand to hand.

'Go on,' he says, 'hold it.'

Before I can say anything, he tips the bucket over my hands. I watch as the elver slides down – and then it is there, in my cupped palms. An elver – yes, an elver – three thousand miles after setting off, turning softly in my hands. It is delicate and light, unimaginably tender and light, and I suddenly laugh at the sheer strangeness of it.

'Those are its eyes,' Andy says, pointing over my shoulder.

At the tip of its head I can see two dots: two pin-pricks of black.

'And that?' I ask, pointing to a small mark below the eyes. There, caught in the transparency of the elver's body, is a dash of red.

'Its heart,' he says.

It floats there, wondrously vital and clear, and I fancy I can see it palpitating, expanding and contracting under the gleam of our torch.

I slip it back into the bucket and watch as it darts around, lifting its head in bewildered inquiry. The river is moving quickly now, urgent in its fullness.

A few minutes later, we hear muffled footsteps down-river, and a man materialises out of the dark. Andy's friend has been fishing a few minutes away from us, and he has come to share the warmth of our fire. They compare catches – Dave has caught twelve elvers to Andy's one – and they both seem excited, although in a gruff, understated way. The first eels have started to run, and they are hoping that hundreds or even thou-sands more will follow in their wake. Fishing five miles downriver, Dave's son has already caught a kilogram of elvers, and there are reports of similar catches elsewhere, at Maisemore, towards the mouth of the Severn, and in the River Parret in Somerset. But things are changing, they say, and talk soon turns to the decline of fishing, to how much bigger the catches were in the '90s, '80s, '70s. The rivers are different now. There are more sluice gates, more dams, more tidal flaps, more concrete and more steel, and what chance do the elvers have against concrete? Andy asks, gesturing towards the river. Dave nods. There's not much we can say to that.

I walk down to the river, where our elver is tracing hesitant circles around the base of the bucket. Its eyes are dark and concentrated, its body graceful and lithe, and it is almost completely transparent, apart from a fine black line running through its length, which I later learn is the beginning of pigmentation. It seems very curious, fascinated by its plastic bucket. But it also seems afraid, unsure of its new world. It wanted out.

Among the banks, the wind shakes the willows, shakes the willows and then stops. And looking at the river, I suddenly feel very small in its presence. I think of all the creatures hidden in its chambers, not only eels, but also salmon and dace, barbel and pike, chub and trout. A whole world was unfolding there, and it was all happening out of sight.

Later that morning, when the fishing is done, we clamber over a tidal gate with all the elvers we caught that night. The gate is operated by remote control, Dave tells me, and is one of the many barriers separating eels from their wetlands. Then they give me a bucket of elvers. Andy and Dave have only caught twenty or so, too few to sell to the fisheries, and so we have brought them here, where they think they will have a better chance of surviving.

We walk down to the edge of a ditch, which runs for miles into the country, and where the water is dark and cold and clear. I crouch down, tip the bucket, and watch as the elvers flutter slowly out, like flakes of snow.

Long after that trip to Tirley, images from the Severn would return unbidden – the elver's heart, the glowing embers, the moonlight on the water . . . For months, too, the world felt roomier, more alive. Suddenly a river in Gloucestershire was connected to the Atlantic, and now there was a direct line between Tirley and the Sargasso Sea.

At the same time, I continued to be troubled by one aspect of my trip to Tirley. It was the news on the radio in the hours before I met Andy and Dave, the scandal of the Windrush generation – a scandal which, as the weeks passed, ramified into a political crisis for the government, as more revelations and insidious policies came to light. I don't want to press the analogy – the life-worlds are incommensurable, for a start; the histories and ontologies too distinct – but there seemed to be a parallel, at least to my mind, between the 'hostile environment' of the government's immigration policies, and the hostile environment we have built for eels. A recent survey by a group called AMBER (Adaptive Management of Barriers in

European Rivers) has counted more than one million human-made obstructions in rivers and streams across Britain and continental Europe. Upon reaching these shores, then, thousands of miles after beginning their journeys, eels face endless barriers obstructing their progress upstream: tidal flaps, weirs, dams, sluice gates, hydropower stations. In the past fifty years, elver populations in Europe have collapsed by 95 per cent.

Politically, materially, ecologically, Britain resembles a fortress at times. Lodged in the economic order we call capitalism are deep divisions based on class and race: divisions reified by, and reified in, the country's immigration policies, differences in educational opportunities, and inequalities in wealth. In England, these widening divisions have also gone hand in hand with the development of elite, gated communities around the country, as well as a marked rise in what is known as 'hostile architecture' – design features that deliberately make public spaces less congenial. Wires covering concrete barriers, to discourage sitting, benches tilted at sharp angles, to prevent rough sleeping, as well as spiked ventilation shafts and metal-studded pavements, to ward off the homeless. Meantime, AMBER continues to add more obstructions to the list, while the habitats of countless creatures are disappearing, if not already gone. Britain is losing its birds, bats and toads, its voles, pine martens and butterflies, its beetles, moths and bees. What all this amounts to, it seems, is a failure of care – and sometimes even an embargo on hospitality. In 2016, a convoy of activists travelling to France were stopped at Dover and refused entry to the port. They were carrying food, blankets and other supplies for the refugees in Calais. When food is diverted from the hungry, you know a crisis is at hand – a crisis of politics, of fellow feeling, of spiritual values.

But so much manages to cross borders too: food and money, tents and tools, letters of solidarity, hope. In Bristol, where I live, herbalists gather plants in the spring and the summer, herbs that they turn into medicine in the autumn and later send to asylum seekers and refugees – tinctures and teas, ointments and oils. Now, on the way to work, whenever I see dandelion and yarrow in the verges, or burdock and comfrey in the fields, I recall that nature's bounty is vast, as is the realm of human kindness, and often surprising too. Where some see weeds, others see gifts, and what some regard as empty spaces, others know as places of medicine.

At night, one also knows that the eels are slipping through our tidal defences, crawling through sluice gates, finding their way across weirs. They are persistent and filled with a form of love – the desire to keep existing in this world. For they don't know any world that's better, despite all the obstacles in their way here.

Their ingenuity is also a kind of hopefulness, a hope that the world's roominess, its hospitality, might persist.

The hopefulness is contagious, and it makes our world more spacious too. For eels, among the other things they do, make us reconsider geography. Pulling at the edges of our maps, they stretch them into new shapes, and so reveal borders for what they are − a kind of conceptual putty. The creature is known as the 'European eel', but in fact it is not European at all. It can be found in the rivers of Morocco, Algeria, Tunisia and Egypt. Its range is wide: it likes a broad margin to its life. And why not? After travelling 3,000 miles from the Sargasso, how could it only be content with western Europe, when it might as well go the extra thousand miles to the Nile, or to the rivers of Latvia and Estonia? When I realise this, the different lines running in my mind, from the Severn to the Sargasso, or from the Elbe to the Atlantic, become woven in with other lines, with strands from Algeria and Finland, Norway and Greece, and soon it becomes hard to look at the atlas in the same way. Eels fold the map of the world along different creases, make the planet wider and stranger than the one we knew. But they also knit our world together, bring the Sebaou in line with the Shannon, the Loukkos together with the Loire.

One evening in Bristol, after the workday is done, I walk down to the river. The summer has ended, the nights have been getting shorter, and when I set off, the light is already dwindling. I point my nose towards the water, walk down busy roads, past a Victorian cemetery, down steep hills, and it isn't until I reach sight of the river that I realise something curious: that I am not so much directing myself as being guided or pulled. I begin to understand, without articulating it, that I have come for the eels, to witness what I cannot see, their underwater migration towards the Sargasso, where they breed and then die. The air is cold by the river, but the ground retains a little of the day's heat, and I watch as night comes over the Avon. The river is heavy with water, water that seems to come on with great strength and without end, and for a moment it seems as though the river were being fed from an imperishable source, from a fountain deep within the earth, and I know that the eels are running now, at this very moment, in Bristol, Lille, Gdańsk.

Hydraulics

ELLENA SAVAGE

A few weeks before I moved alone from Athens to Birmingham, a city once described by the band Black Sabbath as 'the cultural armpit of Britain', my habitually clenched jaw, a condition called bruxism – an old companion – evolved into a dental emergency. The filling in my number 1 posterior molar (the first, or last, tooth in my upper-right jaw) was cracked and the tooth had come loose, leaving the root disturbed and prone to infection. I went from not knowing the meaning of 'dental abscess' to knowing it.

My young dentist, Michalis, is a scrupulous and ambitious person with the nervous posture of someone on the brink of a breakthrough. I trust him. I think of myself as an ambitious person, too, possibly ripe for a breakthrough. Or at least I, too, am nervous. While he slowly corrected the deep-historical dental misfortune bestowed on me, Michalis told me about the secrets of dentistry and the fluoride content of natural waterways. While repairing my bruxism wound, he convinced me to purchase a four-hundred-euro retainer to protect what was left of my choppers. I did as he said. I handed him the money. The dental guard would take four uncomfortable sessions to fit, during which Michalis would shave micro-millimetres off a resin cast of my upper teeth to perfectly fit my bite.

During these sessions, when Michalis's hands were not in my mouth, we talked about the UK, where Michalis had trained and where I had been offered a year-long contract to teach creative writing. Before I answered the job ad, in the midst of a crisis of self-esteem during which I wailed uncharacteristically and inconsolably while washing the dishes, walking the dog, watching TV, I had not once considered living in the UK. I had a passport and some relatives living in northeast England, but the prospect of living there had never occurred to me. Britain remained in my imagination the sad, impoverished place from which my grandmother had fled to Australia with her children in tow, never to return. A place of cruel class hierarchies; a place that could not face its hideously violent colonial history and so suppressed knowledge of it entirely, and

– I was abreast of the news; the UK was up shit creek without a paddle! – all this had been for *what*, exactly?

Indeed, this is not an uncommon perspective for a non-British person. Many of us are baffled by Great Britain's story of its exceptionalism. And yet the island's enduring power is undeniable; the structure of its logic – the logic of gentlemanly capitalism, concealing the filth of production and hoarding its profits – is pernicious and unavoidable, wherever you live. What was it, Michalis and I wondered, about this small island that made its people so set on conquering the globe? What did they want? On the individual level, we conceded, the people tended to be very friendly, and we both appreciated the energy they invested in cultivating their humour. They were not individually responsible for whence they came, just as one is not responsible for one's dreams. And yet as an idea, Michalis and I thought, Britain was one we could do without.

If I were to apply the same question to myself, there in the dental clinic – *what did I want?* – I am not sure I could have answered honestly. I did not want to leave my partner or my seven-month-old Chihuahua mix, Sock, with whom I was obsessed. Or did I? I did not want to move from my comfortable apartment to a bedroom in a stranger's flat to work a demanding full-time job, one that would definitely delay the completion of my novel. *Or did I???* I wanted to use my capabilities, yes, I wanted to test and cultivate the resources of my personality, and I wanted to feel needed (no writer is ever really needed). But perhaps it was not that complicated after all: I needed a paycheck, and I would not get it in Athens.

To counteract the stress of this extreme life I had apparently chosen, I consoled myself with fantasies of being a 'liberated intellectual lady writer' when I arrived alone in the Second City. My new job was not yet another insecure contract in my long history of insecure contracts, I told myself; it was a *residency*, albeit one with an unusually heavy teaching load. It would be a break from my frivolous social calendar and the domestic negotiation that is wedlock. When I was last footloose and fancy-free – almost a decade ago – I had been too poor and wretched to make good use of my freedom. I saw it then as a burden. Now with an income, the wisdom of better habits, and a university library card, I imagined late nights of study, sorting through piles of marginalia in the special collections. I imagined writing arcane little essays from the dustbins and winning minor literary fame in the meantime.

Three days before I was due to leave Athens, our puppy Sock, who had been unwell, went for a spinal tap to test for meningitis. The vet called me while I was in Michalis's surgery to tell me he wasn't waking up from the anaesthetic. Over the coming days, Sock would cycle in and out of consciousness and he would not eat. My partner Dom and I would stay up all night with his tiny, weakened body; we would rub honey onto his gums to increase his blood sugar levels; we would transport him in his beloved dog bag to our local vet clinic and home again, and then in taxis from the vet clinic to an outer-suburban vet hospital that charged several hundred euros a night to monitor him. Sock would soil himself, he would collapse, we would wipe him clean and kiss his terrified face. We would soothe him like one would soothe a baby, our baby, and then we would engage in charged, expensive, verbal battles with veterinarians. They had missed something, we said, they had to fix it. I could not accept that this tiny, beautiful creature, my son, was dying, and I had to teach on Monday.

I boarded my flight and was immediately struck by a soaring sense of guilt, one which would not leave me for months. I was away, and Dom alone would care for Sock's precarious life. I was away, and when it happened, Dom alone would deal with Sock's death, the small body, the bills. When he called me at 5 a.m.

that Friday, I was already awake, as if waiting to hear it, as if my body knew.

In the bed of my rented room, I cried for three days and nights and did not get up. Outside my window, the reservoir swelled with fresh rain. Geese honked. Grass sprouted. It was green and grey and the whole semester was tainted by my sorrow. I wrote my lectures; I read my readings; I answered my emails. After work, I lay on my side and watched *Grey's Anatomy*. I suspended my plans to become the lady Walter Benjamin of Birmingham and accepted my reality, which was that I was just another tired teacher thinking about the contents of her fridge.

That semester, I felt more alone in the world than ever before. I felt that way because in fact it was true; I was alone, truly and completely. Weeks passed during which my only human contact was with students almost half my age. I messaged acquaintances and friends of friends and one by one they cancelled our dates. I submerged myself in the duties of my job such that when I did receive a rare invitation, I was often too exhausted to embark on the challenge of conversing with a stranger who might or might not like me. To distract myself from the encroaching belief that I might not exist at all, I walked long distances around the city with audiobooks blaring in my ears. I believed I was still open to beauty, surprise and friendship, but beauty, surprise and friendship were repelled by me.

And so my first encounter with Birmingham's canals (more mileage than Venice) was a happy one – I had not expected them to be so pretty. I took photos of their glassy surfaces, which reflected the towers looming above, and of the elegant narrowboats nesting at their banks, which had romantic names like Papillon, Rune, and Neptune. Sometimes, when I retreated into my vacant grief, I forgot I was walking just inches from the water's edge, and if I tripped I might fall right in – the still surfaces were so unreal they appeared like solid panes of marble extending out from the pavement. Why were they, fluid bodies of water, so still? I thought. Something about hydraulics, I thought. Something about logistics, I thought, and immediately, I felt bored.

Obviously, I knew nothing – less than nothing – about canals.

Whenever I was struck by some new canal feature on my walks, a feature I knew nothing about, not even the correct words with which to describe what I was seeing, I found myself caught between a desire to learn about canals and alleviate the shame of my ignorance, and an infantile resistance to any and all technical information. I am habituated to finding such facts mind-numbingly dull; a wound from childhood, of course.

When I think back on my early life I'm met with endless scenes of such boredom; me staring out of a car window while my dad and two brothers recite and dispute 'facts' about trains, planes, coal steam power stations and ball-bearings. Yes, ball-bearings. What's a ball-bearing? What's a 'crank'? How do you guys *know* all this random crap? Such questions were not permissible in this house of dismembered information, lest they expose the questioner's ignorance. And the only girl! What was I to do but occasionally intercede with false opinions on matters that felt to me corpse-like and inert; *sharks* cannot! *swim upstream, fact!* No, I have never cared about the sound barrier nor the names of the first pilots who broke it (though tragically I do know their names: Chuck Yeager; George Welch). To the contrary, I cared only about the human heart's boundless capacity to inflict and endure betrayal – a subject that 'conveniently' never came up on long car-drives, unlike river networks or radiation poisoning. To this day when I sense a naked fact, a fact without consequence, human context, or at least some jazzy, literary theme attached to it coming my way, my body goes rigid and I get the chills. I feel like dropping to my knees and lowering my cheek to the rough pavement: *is it over yet?*

Which is to say: logistics . . . No thank you! If we must talk about highways, let us talk about the highway's metonyms: Lana Del Rey's pot-bellied Harley daddies, serial killers, ladies of the night in shiny red cowboy boots. Highways might transport white goods, but we will talk about them in terms of the great American conflation of mobility with freedom! If we talk about ships, please refrain from mentioning hulls or knots. How about instead we discuss the carrack of the early Modern period and then the full-rigged ship as symbols of the contradictions of the Enlightenment??? Pirates *and* the enslaved. Colonisation *and* mutiny. Displacement *and* adventure. The towering will of the ocean *and* the terminal persistence of little human creatures. Freedom from the abusive romance of origins *and* scurvy!

These were the thoughts that began turning in my head when I thought about canals. All the transport modes belonging to the Modern era are drenched in cultural metaphors. Or so I believed. I was probably so ignorant about canals, I thought, because my local cultural touchstones growing up in Australia were river- rather than canal-based. What was a canal, really? My obliviousness was so deeply ingrained I remembered once describing Berlin's Landwehr Canal as 'the lagoon'. If I wanted to learn the story of canals, rather than just the technical details, I would have to sort through the cultural references and metaphors. Only then would I understand the pulsing heart of these aquatic highways, the hopes and dreams they embodied, and the contradictions they exposed.

The first metaphors that came to mind were 'love canal' and 'birth canal'. Then, after a consultation with a Birmingham dentist about another dental abscess, 'root canal'. Disgusting metaphors, all. I dug a little deeper and found one instance of the line 'Speech, thought's canal!' in a poem from 1742, but this clearly this did not take off; it is an entirely repellent metaphor. I asked my pro-logistics friends what they knew of canals and they all said more or less the same thing, that canals were an important part of early industrial history – but this I had already worked out on my own. Thanks for nothing!

For a mode of transport so central to the industrial revolution – canals more or less enabled the transport of goods from town to town in England and elsewhere for the first time – they feature curiously little in the culture. They should have a whole expanding catalogue of contradicting meanings and misappropriations. To the contrary, the presence of canals in the culture seems to be as a dumping ground for shopping trolleys and for bodies, and an otherwise nice place to walk on a Sunday. Online I read that Manchester's canals regularly brought up human corpses, an alarming fact, but not one to worry about, said the article. The bodies did not seem to be connected to one another. But I was worried. I was scouring for an argument about canals, one I could either accept or challenge, but all I could dredge up were loose, disorganised facts. Canals had been totally domesticated, I thought, they were like a mark on the wall that the whole family could no longer see. And if something right in front of you seems at the same time to be invisible, it may be that the invisibility is concealing something horrid.

I considered that the lack of imagination around canals could be a result of their function as a network for transporting goods, rather than people, and so the 'cultural' aspect of the transport system remains under-developed (goods tend not to return from their journeys with stories to tell). The other transport modes – ships, highways, planes, trains, horses, cars, skateboards, etc. – connect people with their desires, stretch their inner resources and at times deliver them to their gruesome fates. They move people to sites of conflict, encounter, hope, tragedy, romance and difference, and these are the scenes that shape the dramas of the world.

As I conducted my admittedly ad hoc and amateur review of Britain's canals' cultural history, I learnt that canals are not only the world's prettiest if most boring unit of logistics. They also tell us about the cruel foundations of British exceptionalism. People have been cutting canals for irrigation ever since there have been crops. During the thousands of years between the first canals and the first Industrial Revolution, short canals were used around the globe for drainage and short-distance transportation. The 'canal age', however, erupted in the eighteenth century when James Brindley built a level, continuous, ten-mile canal from the coal mine in Worsley to Manchester – a feat of modern engineering – which included an open aqueduct to carry the canal over the River Irwell. Brindley's Bridgewater Canal, completed in 1761, halved the price of coal in Manchester, and after that, canals began popping up everywhere. You could argue that the Bridgewater Canal *is* the first Industrial Revolution. Cheap fuel stimulated production. Goods plundered from the colonies were transported efficiently around the island, feeding and clothing the emerging class of industrial workers. Without these long, straight canals lined with puddling clay – another of Brindley's simple but world-changing technologies – Britain's industrialisation might have had to wait until the advent of the railway, almost a century away. Like every aspect of Britain's economic development, that first act of industrialisation depended on the riches exploited from enslaved labour and colonial plunder. Indeed, the early canals were usually paid for with profits direct from the slave trade, and their barges moved goods produced by enslaved people: cotton, indigo, tobacco, rum, and the tea and sugar that fuelled the organs of factory labour.

It wasn't long before I developed another dental abscess. The random dentist I found near my campus, a brusque older man I imagined was saving up for a yacht, told me if the medication didn't take, a root canal would cost half of what I would earn that month. It would wipe out my very reason for being in 'the Venice of the North' in the first place – to collect my pay cheque and continue writing my brilliant, if largely unwritten, novel. I hit the internet to find another solution and learnt that masseter Botox was better than anything for bruxism. Immediately I typed *botox near me* into my phone and discovered there were more cosmetic-injection clinics in my neighbourhood than cafés, newsagents and corner shops combined. The bonny lass at Studio Aesthetika injected me on the spot and even gave me a discount. She told me I had really soft hair. Ten days later, at my aftercare appointment, she did not know who I was – she'd lost the form I'd filled out the previous time – but happily topped up my jaws for free. I thought about how far I had travelled

– descended? – these past few months, how we were all simply effects of economic relations, the longue durée of merchant capitalism had led us all to exactly where we currently stood – or lay, splayed out on an aesthetician's bed as she injected a neurotoxic protein into my jaw. I had few friends within a thousand-mile radius, no dog, no lover, I was haggard and tired and my teeth were – literally – ground to a (dental) pulp. On the upside, the Botox was cheap. I considered getting my whole face done.

After some time living this fragmented life, I became accustomed to it. I found a place to live in, with people in similar circumstances to my own. I befriended my colleagues, despite their resistance. I worked, I got paid, I bought a pair of blue loafers and a good woollen coat that fit well. One afternoon in early spring I walked home from work in my dandy outfit along the Worcester and Birmingham canal. In the grass at the edge of the water, I saw a man and a boy, his son. The man had one leg stretched out in front of him and the other curled at his side. He propped himself back on his elbow and looked out softly at the water. The kid was catching insects in the grass with a small net. I imagined they lived on one of the narrowboats. The scene could have been from any afternoon in spring in the last four hundred years, or so I liked to imagine. I took a surreptitious photo 'of a swan' (who did not like the attention) and caught the man's outline at the edge of my frame. I walked on. The light was such that the water's surface was not visible at all, only the shattered reflection of heaving poplars and the blue sky.

Beyond the River

Rumer Godden's
The River

TESSA HADLEY

The only thing I don't like in Rumer Godden's 1946 short novel *The River* is the first paragraph; every other word in the book feels right. In her first paragraph Godden writes that although 'the river was in Bengal, India . . . for the purpose of this book, these thoughts, it might as easily have been a river in America, in Europe, in England, France, New Zealand or Timbuctoo, though they do not of course have rivers in Timbuctoo . . .' I wonder why she began with that disclaimer. Because everything that's marvellous in *The River*, it seems to me, has to do with its precise evocation of one particular place at one particular moment in time, which feels so exact and so true.

It surely isn't right that a story that happens in one place and at one moment can be transposed and put down in another place and moment, without being changed utterly. The where and the when in prose fiction are everything, they are the conditions that give rise to both the story and its form – even in science fiction and fantasy.

The River is the story of an Anglo-Indian family in a small town beside the mile-wide Brahmaputra river in what was then India and is now Bangladesh; Anglo-Indian in the sense of being white, British-born and living in India, when it was still part of the British Empire. The father of the family manages a jute works, set among fields where the jute is grown; the plants are carded and cleaned and graded ready for sending down the river to the mills in Calcutta, where they will be turned into matting and hessian cloth and rope. Godden herself grew up in similar circumstances, except that her father managed the steamboats on the river. And just as the family's story couldn't be set anywhere else, it isn't timeless either. Godden tells us that the children haven't 'been sent away out of the tropics because there was a war; this war, the last war, any war, it does not matter which war'; but everything in this writing is feeding us the economic and cultural specifics necessary to grasping this particular moment of Empire, global manufacture and trade. Although

Jean Renoir's 1951 film adaptation sets *The River* in the early forties, the world of the novel surely belongs rather to the years of Godden's own childhood in the First World War. We know at any rate that it's a time when, under normal circumstances, an Englishman living in India sent his children 'away out of the tropics'. All of the displacements of Empire are registered there, the fault lines of consciousness in an imperial ruling class, their being in the place but not of it.

The story is told through the Englishman's daughter Harriet, who's on the brink of adolescence. She lives in the Big House attached to the jute works, along with her older sister Bea, younger brother Bogey, and toddler Victoria – and their many servants. 'Nan was a Catholic; Abdullah, the old butler, was a Mohammedan, and so was Gaffura his assistant; Maila, the bearer, was a Buddhist from the state of Sikkim; the gardeners were Hindu Brahmins, Heaven Born; the sweeper and the Ayah were Hindu Untouchables and Ram Prasad Singh, the gateman, the children's friend, was of the separate sect of Sikh.' It has to be one of the children who tells this story. The children's parents are loving and sympathetic enough, yet they can't see the whole world of this river community which their children can see. They're too fixed in their type and their class, too decently and drily English, their perspective is too limited. The children can look bluntly, so to speak, with open eyes; they aren't fixed in their roles yet, they can see what their parents choose not to see. They know their way intimately round all the stalls and sights of the bazaar; Bogey knows there's a cobra living among the roots of the peepul tree in the garden. Beyond their sheltered lives inside the routines of the Big House, with its European values and education system, they have childhood's free pass to come and go from the Indian community which is the only outside world they know.

Vividly they see the racial differences according to which their world is divided up. Little Victoria is 'very plump, very blonde, built into a beautiful heavy pink and pearly fleshed body'; at this phase of her life, she's inseparable from old Nan, who is 'thin, small, very dark, with a fine brown skin that was slack and tired now and showed bluish shadows and pouches under her eyes'. Nan's hands are 'small and thin and busy, and her fingers were wrinkled and pricked at the tips with a lifetime of washing and sewing'; Harriet often discounts Nan, partly in the racialised perceptions of their world – Nan doesn't count, she doesn't matter. Yet so often it's Nan who supplies the crucial touch or significant word which nourishes the children and guides them; their own mother is kind and sensible but somehow remote from their intimate lives. Bea is excruciated when their mother talks to her and

Harriet about menstruation. 'We women have to make our bodies fit for [childbearing] ... like a temple' she says, in her enlightened bright English voice. Like a *temple*? Harriet responds, surprised: unlike her mother, she's surely thinking of a Hindu temple, the only kind she knows. The children can't see Nan because she's everywhere, she's their horizon ('Nan was Nan ... like bread, too everyday and too necessary to be regarded'); but the novel brings the nurse and the baby close together at the end of their descriptive passage, in a relationship deeper at that moment than any race difference. Nan's 'eyes were like Victoria's, brown and clear; as her body receded it seemed to leave all her life in her eyes'.

Although they know that their mother wouldn't allow it, Harriet and Bogey watch the funeral pyre of Ram Prasad's young wife, hiding behind a brick kiln on the edge of the burning ghat. 'Did you mind it?' Harriet asks Bogey afterwards, but he says he didn't. 'It looked just like burning to me.' After the burning, the ashes are given to the river, 'a great slowly flowing mile-wide river between banks of mud and white sand, with fields flat to the horizon, jute fields and rice fields under a blue weight of sky. "If there is any space in me," Harriet said, when she was grown up, "it is from that sky."' Harriet struggles, in the story, with the passing of her childhood. She still has dirty scratched knees, and her dress is stained and torn from playing with Bogey; but her body is changing and she's full of anguished questioning about time, and death, and self. Her sister Bea seems to manage growing older with such grace; why can't she be the same? She sees the shape of Bea's face, 'oval and clear, with the clear modellings of the cheekbones under their soft skin, her straight small nose and the fine lines of her eyebrows' and asks her mother if she is as beautiful as Bea. '"You have a little face full of character," her mother says. That means I am not, thought Harriet.'

The novel is almost, but not quite, a story of first love. Captain John, tortured and young and with an artificial leg, comes to stay with them at the jute works, bringing his dreadful message from the European war. At first the girls are repelled by his suffering, they hate it. '"I don't want to think of Captain John," said Harriet with a feeling of fixed hard naughtiness. "Why should there be a Captain John?"' But as the novel progresses they're both drawn to his darkness as well as to his intelligence, as if there's something in it they need to know. It's Bea he's attracted to, and half-uneasily she likes him in return, but Harriet also agonises over the captain. He reads the poetry she writes and takes it seriously, and mostly it's just that serious attention she wants from him; distracted by Bea, though, he tells Harriet to stop tagging on to him all the time.

'"I hate him, I hate him," said Harriet again, crying into the floor ... "I warned you," said Nan.'

Yet all the time while we're following this familiar, poignant story, the real heart of the novel is elsewhere: in Bogey, the boy who (like Kipling's Kim) has been absorbed so far into the reality of India that, although he's English and white, he doesn't want to belong to that white world any longer. Bogey's been allowed to run free in the garden of the Big House and beyond it. He refuses to learn to read, he isn't interested in spellings or history, and is absorbed by the insect and animal life in the garden and outside; he eats ants to make him wise, never tells anyone when he hurts himself, and doesn't even want Christmas presents – when he's given lead soldiers, he only buries them. 'He was not capable of being made to feel guilty ... he simply removed himself'. '"One day you will have to learn to read," said Harriet. "Imagine a man who couldn't go to the office, nor sign letters, nor read newspapers." "I am not going to be any of those men," said Bogey', who is still in that crucial passage of free play, in between dependent babyhood on the one hand, and on the other an initiation into adult culture. When he watches the snake charmers in the bazaar he sees the kind of adulthood he thinks he wants.

And then a cobra comes to live in the peepul tree, which grows half in the children's garden and half

outside it; using the tin whistle given to him by Captain
John, Bogey tries to tame it. Because he's adept in his
world of nature, and because there's an English tradi-
tion of boys running wild in their childhood, exploring,
making fires and taking risks, his family have trusted
that Bogey knows what he's doing; the reader has
trusted too. (Of course his family – apart from poor
Harriet – don't know about the snake, and the children are supposed to tell their father if ever they see
a snake inside the garden.) But Bogey doesn't really
belong inside any Indian culture, he's just a little white
boy at play, dreaming, making up snake charming all
by himself, alone, out of his ignorance, and one afternoon while the family sleeps, the cobra kills him. The
children's Ayah, who figures far below Nan in their
hierarchical world, tells Victoria the forbidden terrible
thing, the thing they all dread to know, and have to know:
'"I don't want to see him," Victoria said. "Ayah says he
is all black."' Harriet knew already: when she found his
body in the garden, even before she began screaming
for Ram Prasad, she 'looked and looked and looked'.

I do understand after all, I think, why Godden
began her novel with that disclaimer, claiming that the
story of her novel could belong anywhere. She wanted
to evade that heavy burden of responsibility which can
fall so numbingly on a writer's shoulders; she wanted
her story to take place in a fictional nowhere, so that

she didn't have to answer explicitly to history, and to the vastness of empire and its wrongs, and war. She needed to free herself to tell the subjective truth of her small story exactly, unencumbered. And yet it does feel as if Bogey's death gathers up into its violence some tiny portion of the whole hovering violence and wrongness of that world beside the Brahmaputra River, in its moment of war and empire. Someone has to pay, inside the ethical organisation of the novel; something has to hurt, so that the story doesn't merely register as an idyll, a nostalgic paradise.

This is an exquisite novel – exquisite because every word is hard and exact and perfectly right, not because it's high-flown or prettified; its India isn't veiled in any mystical 'otherness'. Renoir's film adaptation is a marvel too. Perhaps the foregrounded family story isn't woven quite so seamlessly into its Indian world as it is in the novel; there's a stylistic disjunction between the period awkwardness of the performances, and the magnificent documentary footage of the river behind them, complementing Godden's own descriptions of the abundant life of the great river. 'The river emptied itself, through the delta, into the Bay of Bengal, its final sea. There was life in and over its flowing; an indigenous life of fish, of crocodiles and of porpoises that somersaulted in and out of the water, their hides grey and bronze and bubble-blue in the sun; rafts of water hyacinths floated on it and flowered in the spring. There was a traffic life on the river; there were black-funnelled, paddle-wheeled mail steamers that sent waves against the bank and other steamers towing flat jute barges; there were country boats, wicker on wooden hulls, that had eyes painted on their prows and sets of tattered sails to put up in the wind; there were fishing boats, crescents lying in the water, and there were fishermen with baskets, wading in the shallows on skinny black legs, throwing fine small nets that brought up finer-length fishes shining in the mesh.' The river is always flowing close at hand, in the film and in the book, urging its perpetual under-note of change and impermanence, reminding us how experience is multiple, amazing, unfixed and fluid.

Falling Out of the Sky

CALEB AZUMAH NELSON

It's summer again, so you're making what has become a yearly pilgrimage to Andalusia and to this little stretch of sand in particular, which sits so close to the south-ernmost tip of Spain that on clear days, Morocco winks in the near distance. Where the locals don't make any concessions for your lack of fluency, but do encourage you to try again, try again. Where, even in summer, the sun doesn't rise until 8 a.m., and in the hours before that, the sky is jewelled with constellations.

Usually, you and a friend and their family – yes, you've become an add-on to the family holiday – will fly to Gibraltar, make the strange walk across the border from British soil to Spanish, then the hour's drive down to El Palmar. But in 2016, you fly solo to

Seville, where you'll catch the coach coastwards. In the minutes before you land, you gaze through the window, out at a neatly ordered city, split by a long, narrow body of water.

A few hours in the city are enough to encourage a return; nothing more than a feeling, like when you're ineffably drawn to someone or something or some place, unable to explain it, but the feeling is there. The feeling remains, asking you to approach, confront, surrender. Winding through the Andalusian countryside, you make a promise to yourself to return. The following year, you do.

Down by the coast, there's usually a breeze, and if not, when the sun sits high in the sky, there's always the water to run into for some reprieve from the heat. You foolishly assume that August in Seville will bring the same gift, that some magic wind will make its way through the city as the temperature climbs up throughout the day.

After a few hours wandering along pedestrian pathways, the streets quiet in the mornings, it becomes clear that being outdoors is only bearable before midday, or after 6 p.m. Still, you feel the makings of a nice routine: tostadas for breakfast in the restaurant below your apartment, meandering between tall buildings and through narrow walkways before the sunshine's glare becomes too much, then seeking refuge indoors until the sky begins to darken and the city begins to busy itself, and you can re-join the masses spilling out of restaurants and tapas bars.

Seville, even after a day or so, is a welcome break from London, where increasingly you are being coded as dangerous or threatening, and are spoken for before you can speak. In the afternoons, you sit on the balcony of the apartment, and try to find words for this feeling: this grief that comes with your identity being assumed for you, with the loss that lingers when your life becomes an assumption. With a notebook splayed open, you write until the sentences begin to slow, until your mind becomes muddy with the heat, and after a small lunch, collapse on the bed with earphones still trailing from your ears. It's 2017, you're still discovering the depths of Kendrick's lyrics, or rediscovering Dilla's steady and irregular beats, his internal rhythm slowing your own down, towards that place somewhere between waking and sleeping where haze might gain form, where errant thoughts and desires might be clutched and considered. In this instance, it's that long, narrow body of water you glimpsed as you swooped down into Seville. And it's not just the water, but what it might bring for you: a moment to be still, to be present, to be with yourself. When you wake, you make the decision to head towards the river for dinner.

M, whose apartment you're staying in, spreads a map across the dining table, and runs her finger along the river's markings. You lean in, seeing its name for the first time: River Guadalquivir. She points to where you are and draws a straight line from the apartment to the river. The confusion must show on your face, so you explain: it's so close. She shrugs and nods, before pointing out her favourite restaurant, drawing a circle around the area you should stay in, the edge of her pen spilling into the water. Here, she says, repeating herself, stay here.

The rest of the city must have had the same idea: as you make the short walk, surprised that you have not come across the river on your wanders, each place M suggested is full. You manage to snatch a bar seat for a quick bite in one place, before grabbing an ice-cream – always a dulce de leche – from next door, clutching the cone as you head towards the river.

It's not clear at first how to make your way down to the walkway alongside the river, but after a series of twists and turns, you emerge onto the riverbank. The sky above is still blue, with barely a whisper of the coming night's darkness; the energy of the surrounding groups of twos and threes and more reflects this, as they sit and drink and smoke and speak and laugh. It's as if, after the siesta, the day has begun again.

You approach the water's edge, take a perch, let your legs dangle over the bank. The water is still, barely a ripple across its surface. You let out a breath, not realising you have been holding it in and, leaning as far as you dare, try to glimpse your own reflection – but it's too dark. Beside you, there's a group talking loudly over a portable speaker, the beat reverberating out and around as they pass around a neatly rolled joint, the laughter as someone inhales too much too quick and doubles over in a coughing fit.

As the song changes, two of the group start up a heated discussion, which doesn't sound like the first or last time it'll happen, and you have to stifle a laugh because you recognise the song – Danny Brown's 'Really Doe' – and the argument – who had the best verse – because you had the exact same one among a group of friends earlier in the summer, around this time of evening, on the edge of possibility. Their voices echo into the night and you smile at the specificity, the familiarity. The only woman in the group catches you smiling, nodding to the music, mouthing along to the words. She lifts a curtain of dreads that keep falling across her face and her eyes, which even in the dim of dusk you can see are alight with curiosity, and with one easy movement, she opens up her group, extends the question your way. Your answer – Earl Sweatshirt, you say, it has to be – prompts fresh discussion, more chatter: some argue it's Kendrick, with his dexterity and depth. You're offered the joint, which you refuse; you're offered a beer, which you take, holding it loosely around its neck as the woman, Nicole, speaks excitedly to you. It's then you realise you haven't seen anyone in the city who looks like you and this draw towards each other is not just connection or attraction, platonic or otherwise, but safety.

Your Spanish is good, not perfect, but Nicole is patient with you. She asks where you're from and you say, London, by way of Ghana; she tells you Senegal, but has lived in Seville since she was young. She asks you how long you're here; when you tell her one week, her face breaks into a smile and she invites you to a gathering, a late housewarming of hers. You exchange numbers and the group heads off to dinner. You stay by the river, at the water's edge, sat with this moment, with its stillness and presence, with its possibilities.

You shouldn't cross the river, M says. It's morning and already sunshine is trailing across the room. You've just described the encounter from last night, with Nicole and her group, and the invite she extended to her party tomorrow night. When you show M the address, she shakes her head, pointing to where it is on the map.

Triana, she says, muy peligroso. Very dangerous. Don't cross the river, she says.

Her words ring out around apartment, long after she's left. When you head down to breakfast, you push the food around your plate, trying to understand what lay underneath M's warning. She didn't describe the danger but there was implication about the people, the community; it was only when you described Nicole, when you told her she wasn't Spanish but Senegalese, that 'you shouldn't cross the river' became peligroso, danger. You don't think of yourself as particularly rebellious but knowing that danger is often complex, misused, especially when it comes to communities that resemble yours – Black, African – you head back up to the apartment, grabbing your headphones and a hat to block the sun's glare, heading towards the river, wanting to see Triana in the daytime first. To see what danger might be lurking.

You take the same road you did last night, walking through El Arenal, crossing the river at one of the many bridges connecting one side of the city to the other. Triana arrives quietly, without incident; the bustle of tourists scattered across Seville's streets aren't present here. Instead, mostly residential streets, fewer restaurants and cafés. Young people making their way outside in the late morning or perhaps slinking home after a night out. A gentle slowness to each person you pass, some familiarity in this too; not so dissimilar from the suburbs of south-east London, where you're from, where patches of congested high streets are surrounded by quieter neighbourhoods, streets that sprawl endlessly.

You push deeper into the suburb as the sun quickly ascends. The bottle of water you brought along is soon empty. You pass an older Black man pushing along a shopping trolley full of recycling and he nudges with his eyes at the plastic bottle, thanking you with a wink when you hand it over.

Coming around a bend you're greeted with the glitter of the river once more; you've come full circle. You shake your head, still wondering what M's warning implied; maybe you'll ask her when you get back, press and poke at this notion of danger, of its complexities, its misuse. That's what you're thinking when there's a flash of something small and brown coming to rest at your feet.

You bend down to meet the animal with your gaze. It's a tiny songbird, with speckled wings. It's singing. And there's something to the song, and to the way the bird is lying, that immediately lets you know it is dying. The bird is grieving its life; this is its last music. You don't even hesitate, picking it up, laying it to rest on a bench that sits in the shade of a tree. You give the bird a final glance, before making your way back over the river, the bird's song growing shriller and shriller, more desperate, more faint, as you walk away.

The next evening, Nicole leans against the wall of her apartment as you describe the bird's last song. The space heaves with the excitement of partygoers, the music loud enough that your voice strains as you speak. After a few stuttered sentences, she shakes her head, signalling first with her head towards the door, before taking your hand and leading you out of her apartment, downstairs, where you emerge onto the street.

The night is strangely cool, and quieter than you're used to in Seville. As Nicole lights a cigarette, you begin to walk, mirroring yesterday's wander around Triana. You tell her of M's warning, of Triana's gentleness, of the dying songbird. Nicole smiles sadly, tells you that the birds have been dying here, and only here, in Triana, falling out of the sky of their own accord with no sign of harm; people in Seville have taken this as a bad omen. Nicole wonders if it's more a symptom of an unhealthy environment, if this negative energy is being held in their bodies. Grief is not such a sweet song. That grief, she says, of being assumed you are something you are not, is heavy. You nod, understanding.

You both walk on in a new yet comfortable silence. She lives a few minutes from the river and soon enough, you're there. This time, it's the riverbank opposite where you stood a few nights ago, but on this side, it's deserted. Nicole lights another cigarette and tells you it's always quieter on this side. People don't like to cross the river.

She asks more about London and you tell her the birds aren't falling out of the sky, but that people are disappearing and that communities are being closed in on and that you're feeling breathless, often, in the city. You tell her that, on occasion, you begin to wonder if the danger assigned to you and to her and to those who look like you might be true. You begin to wonder if, in those quiet moments, like those you've found for yourself on this trip, you might hear your own song and it might contain a warning of your own danger, your own threat.

But then, you say, there are moments that convince you otherwise. Moments in which you might meet a stranger and they might offer you a hand in the darkness, in which you might find safety in a knowing gaze, in the understanding of one another.

Nicole smiles at this as the first few drops of a heavy rain fall on your shoulders, plop into the river, send out a quiet ripple. Let's go back to the party, she says. You follow her lead, towards something more for yourself, towards possibilities.

The Contradiction of Cities

JAMAL MAHJOUB

To face the river is to turn one's back on the land-scape: the river road with its dark canopy of thick banyan leaves, the cool breeze that blows by the palace, the vegetation that thrives there in the grey silt and blue water. All of this is a distant memory only a few hundred metres away down what was once known as Victoria Avenue, now Sharia al-Qasr, Palace Road.

Even as the Blue and White Niles come together, merging into the main artery that flows north from here, the capital seems to splinter, fragmenting around the point of confluence. By nature this city is plural, a conglomerate of three towns: Khartoum, Khartoum North (or Bahry) and Omdurman. *Al Asima al-Muth-alatha* – the triple capital. This multiplicity hangs over the city as a stark reminder of the country's nature: diversity, plurality and the potential of unity. This is geography as metaphor.

It continues to duplicate itself, multiplying, spreading outwards in ever-expanding rings into new quarters, neighbourhoods, places that have appeared literally out of nowhere. Houses have sprung out of the ground, mud walls rising up, unfolding themselves from the dust to be dubbed with a host of invented names. This is the shape of Doxiadis's City of the Future. As a metaphor for urban expansion in the twenty-first century, it tells us what is in store for Khartoum. The struggle against indifference, anonymity, the submergence of individuality under a flood tide of demographic growth. This is what most people mean when they talk about change. The torrent of people from out there beyond the horizon, from the great wide nowhere. In the long run, this influx may be the only hope this country has of surviving.

At night you find yourself enmeshed in a transit hub that looms out of the dark. Buses, cars, taxis and minivans churn around trying to find their way, spreading drapes of mineral dust that glitter like murky wings in headlight beams. The city has swollen, overflowing its banks. Out of a sense of wonder, people offer to drive you as far as the Sabalouga Dam to prove to you how far the urban sprawl extends. It is as if they themselves do not quite believe what has happened to their city, what is happening before their very eyes. At independence in 1956, it was less a city than a small town. The population of the entire country was put at ten million. Today, the capital alone rivals that figure.

Night and day, minivans and tiny microbuses hurtle along Africa Road, urgently ferrying people to and from the centre. Crossroads wrap themselves like snarled rope around points of convergence. There are stalls with hot tea and snacks. Oil lamps hiss and two-tone horns sound bursts of exuberance. Jagged fragments of music spill from passing windows. Lively food stalls, roadside vendors and market shacks have materialised to feed the needs of thousands of passing strangers daily. Young boys rush around calling out the destinations of places that have just been invented – you won't find them on any map. They lie further out, quarters you have never heard of until you arrive.

Junctions like this are springing up around the city, jumping off stations before you reach the darkness and all points beyond. The roads trail off into the distance and then drop away abruptly, tarmac giving way to sand. After a short gap, another strip might begin, or not. There are no street lights, of course. It's too soon for that. The only illumination comes from passing cars and the flicker of oil lamps. The new quarters adopt names that reflect the state of the world at the time of their birth. There is Dar al-Salaam and El Fatih, Angola and Mandela, as well as a Naivasha – named after the Rift Valley town in Kenya where the Comprehensive Peace Agreement was signed in 2005, ending the Second Civil War. There is even one called Allah Maafy – meaning 'Allah is not in', or maybe 'God doesn't exist'. In ten years' time, perhaps less, this virtual city will come to define the capital by the sheer volume of its inhabitants. By day this geography of necessity comes to light. A stratigraphy of invention. Dusty waste covered with the ground-down detritus of plastic bags and bottles – flattened and curled like curious seashells. It is constantly growing, a steady, timeless accumulation. Rows of adobe bricks lie baking in the sun. The clay-rich earth is mixed with water and straw and then poured into wooden moulds before being stacked and left to dry. The grey-brown colour matches the landscape, rendering the walls indistinguishable from the earth. You drive towards what looks like nothing, only to find yourself suddenly surrounded, as if a dusty sheet has been whipped away to reveal rows of houses. The western edge of Omdurman is now said to reach almost to the border of neighbouring Kordofan province. Nobody knows what is out there. It all folds into the blurred conglomeration of rumour and fear. Some quarters have been here for over twenty years, but are still not officially recognised as part of the city. They are not connected to the power grid or sewage system and water is delivered by two-wheel donkey cart with a rusty tank on the back.

The fear of the incursion of outsiders, the so-called 'Black Belt' of refugees, dates back more than twenty years. This was the fear that the new arrivals, full of anger towards their Northern rulers, would one day rise up from their shanty towns and take their revenge, murdering the good citizens of Khartoum as they slept in their beds. To counter the spread of mud huts, the newly wealthy, pockets plump with oil revenue, have turned their backs on the horizon. Towers are going up all over the place. Ten, fifteen floors or more, far beyond what the infrastructure can bear. In leafy, residential Souq Two the old villas are knocked down with sledgehammers and gardens laid over as cement skeletons rise into the sky and stay there, unfinished. Everything is done in stages. First you buy the land, then you build the framework. The flats are completed only when they are sold. The two cities, the horizontal sprawl and the vertical spiral, are like diametrically opposed universes.

In 1820 Khartoum was no more than a permanent military camp. It only became the functioning seat of Egyptian rule around ten years later. John Petherick and George Melly, two British travellers who visited the town in 1846 and 1850 respectively, make it clear that Khartoum was a place of considerable importance. Both men noted the primitive architecture, the irregular construction of the town, the narrow, winding streets; a constriction relieved only here and there by empty spaces resembling squares, etc. By 1862, when Sir Samuel Baker passed through, the town was still labouring to redeem itself. He recorded it as a miserable, filthy, unhealthy spot whose economy was driven by the slave trade.

Only twenty years on, another visitor, the South Tyrolean Father Ohrwalder, was struck by the pleasant gardens and shady groves of date palms. Perhaps it was all in the eye of the beholder. With the fall of Khartoum to the Mahdi in 1885, the city was abandoned. Everything of value was ferried across the river to Omdurman, where the Khalifa made his base. The mission house, the arsenal and parts of the palace were all that was left standing. Ohrwalder, a Catholic priest who was held captive for ten years, claimed that the building of opulent houses was forbidden by order of the thrifty Khalifa, who feared that it might lead to people hiding money in them. Houses then were not understood as being something permanent. Traditionally built of mud, they could be abandoned and rebuilt at the drop of a hat, much like the settlements on the city's outskirts today. Anything more solid was viewed with suspicion.

After the Reconquest in 1898, Kitchener set about rebuilding his new city, driving linear streets straight through the rubble. The British deemed Omdurman as hopeless, condemned to remain a rabbit warren, where walls were built 'at every conceivable angle and irregular curve'. The streets broadened and converged with no sense of order; at times they simply gave out into a dead end, big enough in places for a battalion to march abreast and in others barely the width of two people standing side by side. It remained largely unchanged from half a century earlier, when Petherick and Melly, exasperated and suffocating, were lost in the maze that is Africa.

W. H. McLean, author of the first urban plan for Khartoum back in 1910, wrote that a new and splendid city had been raised from the ruins left behind by the Khalifa. By 1960 Khartoum covered an area of seven square miles, with a population of around 15,000, all contained within the loop of the railway line that ringed it to the south and over which it was to spill in the coming years. Those living outside this iron arch outnumbered those within fourfold. Omdurman was the largest bazaar town in the entire continent, containing, according to McLean, 'specimens of most of the North and Central African races'. Khartoum, with its planned streets, remained obstinately 'European'.

Across the river in Khartoum North, Nubians were arriving from the area around Aswan, among them my father's family. They raised the number of inhabitants to around 25,000 officially, although, since the figures were not reliable even then, the real number may have been much higher. In common parlance, Khartoum was the 'office', Omdurman was 'home' and Khartoum North, with its growing industrial area of factories and dockyards, was known as the 'workshop'. The business centre of Khartoum had an Arab and a European market, the Arab being more 'Oriental' than 'African' in tone.

The city was certainly more cosmopolitan in those days. At that point a quarter of the population was made up of Europeans, the rest being Egyptian, Syrian and Sudanese. There was a 'Levantine' sector of rather wealthy traders and businessmen from Syria and Lebanon, and a quarter known as 'Little Greece', which began in Abu Tulieh Avenue and extended west to Victoria Avenue. Here there was a colony of middle-class Greeks, with their clinics and social clubs, shops and grocery stores, bakeries, bars, schools and churches, all serving a sizeable Greek community. There were street signs that added Greek names to the more common Arabic or English names. Today, there remain few traces of the Greek presence. The Greek Orthodox Church is secluded behind high walls and large iron gates, chained and padlocked. More commonly there is Papa Costa's bakery and restaurant, where writers still meet to read their work and talk.

At the furthest extreme of the southern end of the city, across the rail loop, lay the New Deims, a colony of mud houses laid out in a gridiron pattern around two large cemeteries that are still there today. These were low-income families who lived in fairly bad conditions, with underground pit latrines. The transverse streets were built wider than the longitudinal to provide shelter from the prevailing north–south winds. South of the New Deims were shanty towns made of tin sheets and wood where the Fellata, who had arrived in search of work from West Africa (particularly Nigeria), lived in less comfortable conditions. In this context, the current expansion of the city seems, in part, like a continuation of what went on before. The old European sections in the centre have faded out, taking with them the cosmopolitan diversity they represented, while the old dynamic between the classes remains.

Am I trying in some way to define myself through understanding this city? How, then, to describe it? The Incomplete City. The Unfinished City? The Broken City? Of course, it's not one city at all, but fractured. It is defined less as a city than by the rivers that flow through it, giving it life. The rivers divide the capital into three lobes. Perhaps there is a clue in this multiplicity. It is young, compared to Cairo, Baghdad or Damascus. It has no Omayyad architecture, no ancient temples or precious libraries. Two centuries ago there was nothing here but a simple fishing village. An improvised city, growing in the disorganised fashion of today's expanding globalised cities everywhere. Mutating. Out of control. There is no narrative here of metropolitan grandeur. This is not a playground for the wealthy, like Dubai, say. Nor an industrial pole of the world such as Shanghai. It is not struggling to hold onto past glory, as some Western cities are, to avoid being turned into gleaming, decrepit icons, of real value only to tourists and real-estate speculators. To write about the cities of Europe or America is to write of places that, as Toni Morrison puts it, the disenfranchised inhabit but have no claim to. Here there is a similar contest in play, as the new inhabitants arrive to face the country's rulers and lay claim to its future.

The question I keep coming back to, perhaps the real reason I came back here, is: what claim do I have to this city? A shared history? The formative years of my life? A sense of heritage, of belonging? Perhaps, but is that really enough? I didn't come here to find myself, but to come to terms with what this country means to me, and the truth is that all I really know of it is this city. I have always lived in cities. Despite a longing for solitude and nature, rural areas make me nervous. I love the anonymity of the city. The sense of equality it brings. Nobody can fully claim the city because its true nature confronts us daily with our otherness.

We like to think we have a hold on those cities in which we have spent part of our lives, but we don't, not really. If we are lucky we might be able to glimpse some unchanged spirit that remains constant in our lifetime, but even that is largely a product of our own imagination. Cities change just as people change. Much as I enjoy revisiting old haunts, it takes more than a few visits to restore that bond; it takes commitment.

In describing Paris, Baudelaire wrote of the joys of losing oneself in the crowd. In Joyce's Dublin, Bloom notes, 'Everything speaks in its own way.' Here, too, it comes in scraps, fragments, glimpses. I struggle to find a way to hold on to what I see around me, to bring it together, to set it in a frame that holds, not just here, but one that resonates out there in the world. My position is uncertain. Unlike Saul Bellow's Augie March, who declares himself an American with conviction, I have only doubt. That was another age. Augie March's exuberance is contradicted by the alienness of New York in another of Bellow's works; the New York of Mr Sammler is a city that is beyond his control, but that points towards the way the world is today. The subcultures and 'panic waving' colour that wrestle the

city from his grasp are somehow familiar, even com-
forting. This is where Hanif Kureishi's Karim Amir
comes in, 'an Englishman born and bred, almost'. None
of these examples is adequate, none of them quite fits
my situation.

All cities are sacred, rising out of the ground to reach
for the sky. The first settlements were burial grounds;
they began when it became important to preserve
our own presence through our ancestors. We started
to take ourselves seriously. Our passing was worthy of
record. Necropolis. Biopolis. The City of the Dead and
the City of the Living. Wittgenstein once wrote that
language is like an ancient city, a maze of streets and
houses, the old and the new. Perhaps the corollary of
this is that all cities are unfinished stories, trying to
invent a language in which to express themselves.

Richard Sennet, strolling through Manhattan with
Hannah Arendt, observes that the exile's voyage to citi-
zenship entails the loss of the self – the gradual dimin-
ishment of the 'I'. This loss of identity, this commitment
to our new belonging, takes place in the city, the matrix
of modernity, somewhere, as Baudelaire observed of
nineteenth-century Paris, it was possible to become
bored. To the poet, escape from boredom lay before
his very eyes, outside, in the encounter with otherness.
To lose oneself in the crowd was to find one's individuality as a poet. This is the contradiction of cities,

to belong is to be reminded of your outsiderness. To many, of course, this is a reason to fear the city, where one is faced with the possibility of encountering the Other: people who are not like you, who do not look like you do, do not share the same cultural references, or religious beliefs.

In the last three decades, Khartoum has become that place, where the otherness of the country has come face-to-face with itself. An accumulation of evidence of the government's failure to resolve the nation's problems. If in the past Sudan's problems were historically associated with conflicts that were far enough away to be out of sight and thus out of mind, the present situation promises that they are now unavoidable, close enough to touch and smell. Once it was possible to ignore what was happening out there. Now, it is right in front of you, at the crossroads. And there is something about this predicament that is both universal and very modern, a sign of the times we live in.

About the Contributors

Niellah Arboine is a writer, editor and broadcaster from south London. Her work centres on the intersections of nature, politics, culture and identity. Currently, Niellah is the deputy editor at *Where the Leaves Fall* and is an original member of *gal-dem* and the former lifestyle editor. You can find her words in a number of publications including *Guardian*, *iD*, *Vogue*, *Time Out London*, *Independent*, *Dazed*, *VICE* and *ELLE*. Niellah co-hosted the award-winning podcast 'Growing up with *gal-dem*', she was shortlisted for the Nan Shepherd Prize 2021 for nature writing and hosted a documentary for BBC Radio 4 on Black journalists in the UK.

Dr Amy-Jane Beer is a biologist turned naturalist and writer. She has worked for more than twenty years as a science writer and editor, contributing feature articles and more than forty books on natural history before writing *The Flow*, her first book of narrative non-fiction, which won the 2023 Wainwright Prize for nature writing. She is a Country Diarist for the *Guardian* and a columnist for *British Wildlife*. She sits on the steering group of the environmental arts charity New Networks for Nature and the land rights campaign RightToRoam.org.uk, and is honorary President of the national park society Friends of the Dales.

Roger Deakin, who died in 2006, was a writer, film-maker and environmentalist of international renown. He was a founder member of Friends of the Earth, and co-founded Common Ground. He lived for thirty-eight years in a moated farmhouse in Suffolk. *Waterlog*, which was first published in 1999, became a word-of-mouth bestseller, and is now an established classic of the nature-writing canon.

Marchelle Farrell is a writer, medical psychotherapist, and amateur gardener, born in Trinidad and Tobago, but having spent over twenty years attempting to become hardy here in the UK. She is curious about the relationship between our external and internal landscapes, the patterns we reenact in relation to the land, and how they might be changed. Her debut book,

Uprooting, won the Nan Shepherd Prize for nature writing and is published by Canongate.

Tessa Hadley has published eight novels – including *Late in the Day* and *Free Love* – and four collections of short stories, most recently *After the Funeral*. She publishes short stories regularly in the *New Yorker*, and reviews for the *Guardian* and the *London Review of Books*; she was awarded a Windham Campbell prize for Fiction and the Hawthornden Prize in 2016, and the Edge Hill Prize in 2018.

Jo Hamya is the author of the novels *Three Rooms* and *The Hypocrite*. She has written for the *New York Times*, *The Financial Times*, and the *Guardian*. She was born in London, in 1997.

Rebecca May Johnson has published essays, reviews and non-fiction with *Granta*, the *Times Literary Supplement* and Daunt Books Publishing, among others, and is an editor at the trailblazing food publication *Vittles*. *Small Fires* is her first book.

Amy Key is a poet and writer based in London. She is the author of two collections of poetry, *Luxe* (Salt) and *Isn't Forever* (Bloodaxe). *Arrangements in Blue*, her first work of non-fiction, was published in 2023 by

Jonathan Cape (UK) and Liveright (US), and her essays have appeared in *Vittles*, *Granta*, *Vogue*, and elsewhere.

Jamal Mahjoub is a British-Sudanese writer. Born in London, he was raised in Khartoum where his family remained until 1990. He has lived in a number of places, including the UK, Denmark, Spain and, currently, the Netherlands. His novels include *Travelling with Djinns* and *The Drift Latitudes*. Under the pseudonym Parker Bilal he is the author of the Inspector Makana crime series and, most recently, the Crane and Drake series. His latest non-fiction book, *A Line in the River*, was longlisted for the Ondaatje Prize.

Michael Malay is a writer and teacher based in Bristol. He spent his early years in Jakarta, Indonesia, before moving to Australia with his family at the age of ten. He is the author of *Late Light*, a book about migration, belonging and extinction.

Caleb Azumah Nelson is a British-Ghanaian writer and photographer living in south-east London. His first novel, *Open Water*, won the Costa First Novel Award and Debut of the Year at the British Book Awards, and was a number-one *Sunday Times* bestseller. It was also shortlisted for the Dylan Thomas Prize, the *Sunday Times* Young Writer of the Year Award, Waterstones

Book of the Year, and longlisted for the Gordon Burn Prize and the Desmond Elliott Prize. He was selected as a National Book Foundation '5 under 35' honoree by Brit Bennet. His second novel, *Small Worlds*, was an instant *Sunday Times* bestseller on publication.

Ellena Savage (she/her) is an Australian author and scholar. Her debut essay collection *Blueberries* (Text Publishing and Scribe UK, 2020) was shortlisted for the 2021 Victorian Premier's Literary Award and longlisted for the Stella Prize.

Notes

I Felt Sure She Had Gone Down to the River

1. *The Diary of Virginia Woolf: 1936–1941*, ed. Anne Oliver Bell (Middlesex: Penguin Books, 1985), 359.
2. Leonard Woolf, *The Journey Not the Arrival Matters*, 34.
3. *The Diary of Virginia Woolf*, 336.
4. Ibid., 326.
5. Ibid., 326.
6. 'River Ouse may become first in England to gain legal rights' (*Guardian*, 2023).
7. *The Diary of Virginia Woolf: 1936–1941*, 336.
8. Ibid., 17.
9. Ibid., 168.
10. Ibid., 286–7.
11. Ibid., 99.
12. Ibid., 238.
13. Ibid., 248.
14. Ibid., 191.
15. Ibid., 138.
16. Ibid., 106.
17. Leonard Woolf, *The Journey Not the Arrival Matters*.

What Is a River?

1. Richardson, M., Hamlin, I., Elliott, L.R. et al. 'Country-level factors in a failing relationship with nature: Nature connectedness as a key metric for a sustainable future'. *Ambio* 51 (2022): 2201–2213.